NEW YORK COOKS

NEW YORK® COOKS

The 100 Best Recipes From
NEW YORK MAGAZINE

Gillian Duffy

STEWART, TABORI & CHANG
NEW YORK

PUBLISHED IN 2003 BY STEWART, TABORI & CHANG
A Company of La Martinière Groupe
115 West 18th Street, New York, NY 10011

Canadian Distribution: Canadian Manda Group, One Atlantic Avenue, Suite 105
Toronto, Ontario M6K 3E7 Canada

Library of Congress Cataloging-in-Publication Data

Duffy, Gillian.
New York cooks : the 100 best recipes from New York magazine / Gillian Duffy.
p. cm.
ISBN 1-58479-314-7

1. Cookery, International. 2. Cooks—New York (State)—New York. I.
New York magazine. II. Title.
TX725.A1 D82 2003

641.59—dc21
2003050465

The text of this book was composed in Tribute and Din.

Printed in China

10 9 8 7 6 5 4 3 2

Stewart, Tabori & Chang is a subsidiary of

6

GRILLING

7

VEGETABLES
AND SIDES

8

DESSERTS

INTRODUCTION

In 1988, when I first began working on the food and entertaining issues for *NEW YORK* magazine, there was a wide, and for most, an unbridgeable chasm between cooking as it was practiced in restaurants and in the home. Restaurant cooking was alchemy, using techniques and ingredients a home cook could hardly imagine—let alone find at the supermarket. Professional chefs tended to be French, and imperious, if they weren't anonymous. Providing recipes for amateurs was déclassé.

How things have changed. Nowadays, ideas move swiftly from restaurants to home ranges. And a cookbook—or two, or even three—is an obligatory step on the road to chef superstardom. As a result, home cooking has never been as diverse or creative. Sophisticated spices and fresh, flavorful locally grown ingredients are available in most parts of the country. As one of the first magazines or newspapers to regularly print recipes from New York's best chefs, *NEW YORK* played a role in this cross-pollination.

The recipes collected here are a record of that change, of what was being served in New York restaurants and the kinds of dishes that most inspired ambitious home cooks. They're also a reflection of how I like to cook and entertain at home: bold flavors, relatively easy preparation, with a special emphasis on dishes that can be made ahead, allowing the cook to interact primarily with the guests during dinner and not the pots and pans.

Finding a good recipe is not just a matter of tracking down a great dish at a restaurant and taking dictation from a chef. These are artists, after all. Recipes sometimes arrive in illegible handwriting, in French with measurements in grams, or to serve twenty or more. Or they are of the "a little of this, a little of that" variety. In the magazine's test kitchen, we decipher these inspired hieroglyphics, test them over and over, adjusting the quantities and translating them for use in a home kitchen.

Of course, over the years we've come to know a few of our chefs pretty well. One we have followed since 1989 is Tom Valenti, who first came to our attention with his big, bold flavors at the charming French restaurant Alison on Dominick Street. We featured his signature dish—hearty lamb shanks—long before the lowly lamb shank became trendy and appeared on every menu in town. Valenti then moved to Cascabel, and later to Butterfield 81. Finally, much to our delight, he opened his own restaurant Ouest, a popular American bistro on the Upper West Side, where we fell in love with his Sunday-night special—an amazing meat loaf wrapped in bacon and served with an intense mushroom sauce. You don't think a meat loaf can be amazing? Try it. For many of our readers, it was an instant classic.

We were also the first magazine to do a feature story about Mario Batali in 1996, soon after he opened his restaurant, Po, on Cornelia Street. At the time Mario, though already ample of girth, was not yet larger-than-life, a TV superstar with a string of the city's most celebrated restaurants. But his Italian flavors were already oversized, as you'll see in his luscious Lasagna Bolognese (page 62), inspired by his time spent in Emilia-Romagna.

Since New York chefs tend to do time in many kitchens around town, picking up influences and experimenting with new ideas and techniques at each, we've mentioned with each of our recipes the particular restaurant where the chef was cooking at the time the recipe was featured. So Daniel Boulud has a recipe from Daniel as well as one from Café Boulud; Jean-Georges Vongerichten has one from from Vong and one from Jean Georges; and Bobby Flay has several recipes from Mesa Grill and his Spanish-inspired restaurant Bolo.

Many of our entertaining issues highlighted the culinary trends taking place in Manhattan at the time: Cooking from the farmers' market in 1993, the Mediterranean influence in 1994, Asian in 1995, Latin American in 1996, Indian in 1998, and homey comfort food in 2001 after 9/11. Today we seem to have come full circle with the return of the sixties' classics: déjà vu all over again! And of course we couldn't omit an annual update on the grilling front each summer.

With almost 1,000 recipes featured in the entertaining issues to choose from for this book, we found there were many similar recipes with subtle differences. For example, in 1988 we featured Chanterelle chef David Waltuck's heady Provençal Fish Stew served with garlicky aïoli croutons, which he made for friends at home. In the ensuing years we have published several comparable fish stews, all of which I have loved; after preparing and tasting them all again, this one has stood the test of time and is still our favorite French classic.

Another area where we have witnessed tremendous change has been the availability of fresh locally grown ingredients. The arrival of Manhattan's Union Square farmers' market in 1976 changed the way we shop and think. The huge variety and selection of vegetables, and especially fresh herbs, was driven by many of the top chefs working with local farmers who began to grow particular heirloom vegetables, herbs, and fruits for them. As befits the name, it has been a special inspiration for Danny Meyer's Union Square Cafe, whose recipe for Endive Spears filled with Crabmeat Salad can be found on page 17.

It's not just the accessibility of seasonal produce that has changed many of the Asian ingredients, such as cilantro, lemongrass, and ginger, are no longer considered exotic. In fact, River Café chef David Burke's Salmon in Foil with Ginger (page 70) was considered very cutting edge in 1989, when fresh ginger, now a supermarket staple, could be found only in Chinatown or at specialty markets.

These favorite recipes, whether they are a restaurant's signature dish or something a chef likes to cook at home for friends, have also been chosen to cover different occasions when family and friends get together. A spicy one-pot Chicken Posole with Ancho Chilies (from Bobby Flay of Mesa Grill) is perfect for a casual evening with friends. An impressive Roasted Beet-and-Goat Cheese Terrine (from David Bouley of Bouley) followed by a Marinated Roasted Rack of Lamb (from Cyril Renaud of Fleur de Sel) served with Gnocchi Gratin (from Thomas Keller of Rakel) is suitable for a more elegant gathering. Of course, Thanksgiving has been featured several times, and we could hardly leave out a recipe for the most celebrated meal of the whole year. After testing many different methods for cooking the "big bird," we felt confident when we featured step-by-step instructions from Waldy Malouf (chef of the wood-fired roasting and grilling restaurant Beacon) for his Perfect Brined Herb-Roasted Turkey—the ultimate method for a foolproof, deliciously moist bird (page 86), which includes his updated version of a traditional sausage-and-apple stuffing.

I have been at pains to avoid complication, testing recipes to ensure that they are straightforward and rewarding for the average home cook, to be shared and enjoyed with friends. I hope that some of those often-clipped-out favorites from over the years that have been included in this book will become favorites anew.

Tuna-Wasabi Wonton (page 14)

TUNA-WASABI WONTON

FROM JEAN-GEORGES VONGERICHTEN *OF* JEAN GEORGES

Cocktail parties needn't be fraught with agonizing details, time-consuming labor, and elaborate multistep maneuvers. Or so we learned when Jean-Georges Vongerichten volunteered this simple, savory recipe. Despite his well-earned reputation as a tireless innovator, the resourceful chef isn't above taking shortcuts like buying premade wonton skins for the base of his Asian-flavored hors d'oeuvre. After the skins are cut and baked, he adorns them with a cream-cheese-and-wasabi paste, pickled ginger, a thin cube of raw tuna, and a decorative sprinkle of sesame seeds. It couldn't be easier. Mastering the art of cocktail-party conversation—that's a different story. YIELDS 24 PIECES

. INGREDIENTS .

24 wonton skins
One 8-ounce tuna steak, about 1 1/2 inches thick
8 ounces cream cheese
2 tablespoons wasabi paste

Juice of 1/2 lime
Salt
1/2 cup pickled ginger
1/4 cup white sesame seeds, toasted

1. Preheat the oven to 350° F.

2. Cut a 2-inch circle from each wonton skin using a cookie cutter. Place the circles on a large cookie sheet and bake for about 5 to 7 minutes, until the wontons look puffy and turn golden around the edges. Set aside to cool.

3. Slice the tuna into 1 1/2-inch cubes and cut each cube into 1/8-inch-thick squares. Mix the cream cheese with the wasabi until smooth, and season to taste with lime juice and salt. Spread a thin layer of the cheese mixture onto the wonton, place a little slice of pickled ginger on top, and finish with a square of tuna. Sprinkle the tuna with sesame seeds.

SHRIMP AND CILANTRO PESTO QUESADILLA

FROM BOBBY FLAY *of* MESA GRILL

When Bobby Flay opened Mesa Grill in the early nineties, he staked his signature Southwestern claim with new-fangled quesadillas filled with everything from garlicky lobster to these zesty cilantro-slathered shrimp. (Why stop there? Think smoked-salmon-and-salmon caviar, goat-cheese-tomato-and-basil, corn and zucchini . . . you get the picture.) Unconstrained by the traditional (often greasy) technique of frying folded-over quesadillas, Flay initially thought of stacking them, club-sandwich-style, and baking them in the oven, producing quesadillas that were uncommonly crisp and light, with a delightful contrast of textures. They work just as well tossed on the grill. They're a cinch to assemble ahead of time, which makes them perfect for entertaining—you might even invite your guests to garnish their own. Cut into eighths for ideal hors d'oeuvres or into quarters for a light lunch. To drink? Margaritas, naturally. YIELDS 1 QUESADILLA

. INGREDIENTS .

Three 6-inch flour tortillas	CILANTRO PESTO
1 cup grated Monterey Jack cheese	1 cup cilantro leaves
1 cup grated white Cheddar cheese	2 teaspoons pumpkin seeds
3 tablespoons Cilantro Pesto (recipe follows)	1 1/2 teaspoons fresh lime juice
Salt and pepper to taste	1 teaspoon minced garlic
3 tablespoons olive oil	1 tablespoon grated Parmesan cheese
1/2 teaspoon ancho-chili powder	Salt and freshly ground black pepper
4 large shrimp, peeled and deveined	1/4 cup olive oil
2 teaspoons sour cream	

1. Preheat the oven to 450º F.

2. Place two tortillas on an ungreased baking sheet. Sprinkle each with the Monterey Jack and Cheddar cheeses, 2 tablespoons of cilantro pesto, salt, and pepper. Stack one tortilla on top of the other, and cover with the remaining tortilla. Brush the top tortilla with 1 tablespoon of olive oil, and sprinkle evenly with ancho powder. Bake until the tortillas are slightly crisp and the cheese has melted, 8 to 12 minutes.

3. Meanwhile, heat the remaining 2 tablespoons of olive oil. Season the shrimp with salt and pepper, and sauté for 2 1/2 minutes on each side.

4. Cut the quesadillas into quarters. Garnish with the remaining tablespoon of pesto, the shrimp, and the sour cream, and serve hot.

5. CILANTRO PESTO: In a food processor, blend all of the ingredients except the olive oil. While the processor is running, slowly add the olive oil. Cover the pesto and refrigerate. (Will keep in the refrigerator for 2 to 3 days.)

ENDIVE SPEARS FILLED WITH CRABMEAT SALAD

FROM MICHAEL ROMANO *OF* UNION SQUARE CAFE

Crabmeat salad has always been a popular appetizer at Union Square Cafe, one of New York's best-loved restaurants. It also happens to be the perfect party food, according to chef Michael Romano, who suggests serving it on endive spears for a particularly elegant presentation. Besides being pretty and easy to eat, it's a study in textural and flavor contrasts: The toothsome crab is refreshingly dressed with tomato water and fresh herbs; the endive leaf adds crunch and mild bitterness, besides being the perfect crab-salad vehicle. Form meets function, to fabulous effect. NOTE: The dressing can be made ahead of time, but the crabmeat and endive salad should not be mixed until ready to serve, as the endive will become limp and may discolor. YIELDS 24 PIECES

. INGREDIENTS .

DRESSING
1 large tomato
1/2 cup mayonnaise
1 1/2 teaspoons Dijon mustard
2 1/2 teaspoons fresh lemon juice
1 teaspoon cognac
1/4 teaspoon kosher salt
1/8 teaspoon freshly ground black pepper
Pinch cayenne
1 tablespoon chopped fresh parsley

1 tablespoon snipped fresh chives, plus extra
   for garnish
1 tablespoon chopped fresh tarragon

FILLING
1 1/2 teaspoons olive oil
1 cup peeled and chopped celery
Kosher salt
4 to 5 large Belgian endives
1 pound jumbo lump crabmeat, picked over
Freshly ground black pepper

1. DRESSING: Place a fine-mesh strainer over a medium bowl. Cut the tomato in half crosswise and gently squeeze the halves, cut sides down, into the strainer. Scoop out any juice and seeds remaining in the tomato, and strain these as well. You should have about 2 tablespoons of strained tomato water. Add the remaining dressing ingredients and whisk well. Set aside.

2. FILLING: Heat the oil in a medium skillet. Add the celery and cook over medium-high heat for 1 minute, until the celery is no longer raw but still crunchy. Season with 1/4 teaspoon salt, and set aside in a bowl to cool.

3. Feel off twenty-four large outer endive leaves and trim the bases. Cut two of the endive cores crosswise into 1/4 -inch slices and toss with the celery. Add the crabmeat and dressing, season with 1/8 teaspoon salt and 1/8 teaspoon pepper, and fold gently with a rubber spatula. Just before serving, mound about 1 tablespoon of the crabmeat into the cut end of each endive spear. Garnish with chives.

CROQUE MONSIEUR WITH CAVIAR

FROM ERIC RIPERT *OF* LE BERNARDIN

Eric Ripert has a flair for fish, to put it mildly: He has elevated Le Bernardin into Manhattan's premier seafood shrine, a compulsory stop on the foodie circuit. The elegant restaurant is French at its core, but the menu reflects Ripert's travels and boundless culinary curiosity. He has even been known to dip into the past for inspiration, as he did when he reinterpreted his grandmother's croque monsieur with a seafood spin. Deconstructing the classic French ham and cheese, he kept the Gruyère but swapped the ham for succulent smoked salmon and gilded the lily with a smattering of Osetra caviar, a sprinkling of chives, and a dash of lemon zest, all sandwiched between slices of buttery brioche. We deemed it the ultimate hors d'oeuvre for our millennium issue, and even though it dresses up delightfully as a special-occasion splurge, it works equally well without the caviar. SERVES 6

. INGREDIENTS .

Twelve ¼-inch-thick slices brioche bread
6 ounces Gruyère cheese, sliced ⅛ inch thick
12 ounces sliced Scottish smoked salmon
1 tablespoon blanched lemon zest

1 tablespoon chopped fresh chives
6 ounces Osetra caviar
¼ pound (1 stick) unsalted butter, softened

1. Place the twelve bread slices on a table. Place the Gruyère cheese on six slices and the smoked salmon on the other six slices. Sprinkle the salmon slices with lemon zest and chives.

2. Divide the caviar and spread over the salmon. Close the sandwiches and butter the outsides.

3. Preheat a sauté pan over medium heat. Add the sandwiches to the pan with the Gruyère side down, and sauté for 2 minutes. Increase the heat to high, turn the sandwiches over, and sauté for 1 minute on the salmon side. Repeat with the remaining sandwiches.

4. Slice the croques monsieurs on the diagonal, or as desired, and arrange them on a plate. Serve immediately.

BRANDADE

FROM ALFRED PORTALE *OF* GOTHAM BAR AND GRILL

The Gotham Bar and Grill is a New York institution, and Alfred Portale, its chef and owner, an avatar of New American cuisine. His signature "tall food" style suits the city with its edible edifices primed to topple at the touch of a fork, but Portale's the first to admit that taste trumps presentation every time. He entertains friends and family at his Hamptons beach house in a more relaxed fashion, and I got a firsthand look at the off-duty chef when he invited a group of us to spend a day with him, fishing and clamming and plundering local farmstands for that night's feast. The biggest hit was a rustic brandade, that Provençal staple of pounded salt cod enhanced with obscene amounts of garlic. Portale mixes flakes of fish into his purée for added texture and achieves a supremely crunchy crust from a topping of bread crumbs, parsley and—yikes—more garlic. For him, the dish might be uncharacteristically flat, but the flavor sure isn't. SERVES 8

·INGREDIENTS·

1 ½ pounds salt cod

2 tablespoons white wine vinegar

1 bay leaf

1 sprig fresh thyme

2 to 3 white peppercorns

2 pounds potatoes, peeled and quartered

½ cup plus 1 teaspoon extra-virgin olive oil

2 teaspoons minced garlic plus 1 clove,
    peeled and minced

½ cup half-and-half

¼ teaspoon cayenne

Coarse sea salt and
    freshly ground white pepper

½ cup fresh white-bread crumbs

1 teaspoon chopped fresh flat-leaf parsley

18 ½-inch-thick slices bread, cut from
    a baguette, lightly toasted

1. Place the cod in a large bowl, cover with cold water, and soak in the refrigerator for 48 hours, changing the water twice a day. Remove the cod from the water and set aside.

2. Place 2 cups of water, the vinegar, bay leaf, thyme, and peppercorns in a saucepan, and bring to a boil. Reduce the heat to medium and add the salt cod. Poach for 8 to 14 minutes, depending on the thickness of the salt cod, until the fish flakes easily when pierced with a fork.

3. Lift the fish from the poaching liquid and set aside to cool slightly. Remove any bones, skin, and gray fat. Break one-third of the fish into flakes.

4. Cook the potatoes in a saucepan of boiling salted water set over high heat for about 20 minutes, until tender. Drain and rice or mash the potatoes. Transfer the potatoes to a bowl.

5. Put the remaining unflaked two-thirds of the cod in a food processor fitted with a metal blade. Add ½ cup of the olive oil and 2 teaspoons of minced garlic, and purée until smooth. Transfer the purée to the bowl with the potatoes and fold together. Work in the half-and-half and cayenne until the mixture is creamy and fluffy. It should have the consistency of mashed potatoes. Season with pepper and fold in the flaked cod to give the mixture texture. Taste and adjust the flavor with a little more garlic and olive oil if necessary.

6. Preheat the oven to 350º F.

7. In a bowl combine the bread crumbs, parsley, 1 teaspoon of the olive oil, and 1 clove of minced garlic, and mix with a fork until crumbly. Season to taste with salt and pepper. Spread the brandade in a 2 ½-quart gratin dish and sprinkle it evenly with the bread-crumb topping. Bake for 20 to 30 minutes, or until the top is browned and the brandade is heated through. Serve with toasted bread.

PINCHO DE POLLO Y CHORIZO (CHICKEN-AND-CHORIZO BROCHETTE WITH CUMIN AÏOLI)

FROM LUIS BOLLO *OF* MEIGAS

Before talented Basque chef Luis Bollo opened Meigas in Manhattan (it has since relocated to Norwalk, Connecticut), he worked in some of the most innovative kitchens in Spain, the three-Michelin-starred Martin Berasategui among them. Now he walks a fine line between the classic and the nouvelle, to delectable effect. The traditional Spanish brochette uses pork and chorizo, but Bollo found that chicken was just as delicious after a soak in zesty marinade. Use imported Spanish chorizo and high-quality Spanish olive oil, and don't stint on the garlicky cumin-spiked aïoli which boldly accents these spicy flavors. YIELDS ABOUT 10 BROCHETTES

. INGREDIENTS .

1 cup mayonnaise
½ clove garlic
1 tablespoon ground cumin
5 to 6 imported Spanish chorizos (1-inch diameter) sliced into ½-inch rounds

3 skinless, boneless chicken breast halves, about 1½ pounds, cut into 1-inch cubes
1 cup Spanish olive oil
12 to 14 bamboo skewers, 8 inches long, soaked in water

1. Put the mayonnaise, garlic, and cumin in a blender and pulse until the mixture has a smooth consistency. Transfer to a bowl, cover, and refrigerate the cumin aïoli. This should be made several hours ahead.

2. Starting and ending with chorizo, thread the skewers with alternating pieces of chorizo and chicken. Set the brochettes in a shallow bowl, cover completely with olive oil, and allow to marinate for 12 hours.

3. Remove the brochettes from the oil and shake off excess oil. Heat the grill or pan until very hot, place the brochettes on the grill, and sear on all sides, turning frequently until cooked through, about 7 minutes. Serve with the cumin aïoli.

GOUGÈRES

FROM TERRANCE BRENNAN *OF* ARTISANAL

Gougères are light and airy cheese puffs made with Gruyère-flavored choux pastry traditionally served as a snack or an hors d'oeuvre with a glass of wine or champagne. As with all fromage-related business, I turned to—who else?—Dairy King Terrance Brennan for this recipe. Brennan, chef-owner of the elegant French-Mediterranean restaurant Picholine, is the man widely credited with turning a town of dairy dilettantes into one now swarming with savvy curd connoisseurs. Picholine's lavish cheese course has become so popular, in fact, that Brennan went on to open Artisanal, a bustling brasserie-cum-fromagerie, the home to some 200 varieties of cheese maturing in the restaurant's own cheese cave. When dining at Artisanal, I can't resist the urge to order a basket of these piping-hot gougères to nibble on while perusing the menu. NOTE: The gougères are best served while still warm. To make life easier when entertaining at home, they can be piped onto a cookie sheet and frozen, then cooked as needed. YIELDS ABOUT 32 PIECES

. INGREDIENTS .

4 tablespoons (½ stick) unsalted butter
¼ cup milk plus extra for brushing
½ teaspoon each salt and ground white pepper
½ cup all-purpose flour, sifted

⅛ teaspoon baking powder
½ cup grated Gruyère plus extra for garnish
2 eggs
Coarse sea salt

1. Preheat the oven to 400° F.

2. In a saucepan, bring the butter, ¼ cup of milk, ¼ cup of water, salt, and pepper to a boil. Remove from the heat and add the sifted flour and baking powder. Stir well and return to medium heat. Cook, stirring constantly, until the mixture pulls away from the sides of the pan and forms a ball, about 2 to 3 minutes.

3. Place the ½ cup of cheese and the milk mixture in the bowl of a mixer fitted with a paddle, and beat until just warm. Add the eggs slowly as the mixer runs, until the dough is smooth and shiny. (Alternatively, stir to cool by hand and beat in the eggs with a wooden spoon.)

Transfer to a pastry bag and pipe in 1-inch mounds using a No. 4 tip, or drop with a teaspoon on a sheet pan lined with parchment paper. (At this stage, the gougères can be frozen and then stored in a plastic bag. They do not have to be thawed before baking, but 1½ to 2 minutes should be added to the cooking time.) Brush with milk and sprinkle with cheese and sea salt.

4. Bake for 10 to 12 minutes; when the puffs are golden-brown, reduce the oven temperature to 375° F and cook for 2 to 3 minutes more. Serve hot or at room temperature. May be reheated.

WARM RED AND YELLOW TOMATO TART WITH GOAT CHEESE SAUCE

FROM WYLIE DUFRESNE *OF* 71 CLINTON FRESH FOOD

When Wylie Dufresne landed on the Lower East Side in 1999, it was as if he fell from the heavens—which, in a sense, he did, having spent the previous seven years toiling in the rarified air of Jean-Georges Vongerichten's restaurants. Dufresne's inventive American cooking at 71 Clinton Fresh Food got noticed right away, and the thirty-seat storefront was packed nightly with curious connoisseurs. Determined to put the wunderkind to the test, we challenged him to create an elegant sixty-minute summer menu that would provide maximum flavor with minimal effort. He succeeded handily, choosing seasonal ingredients and replacing laborious sauces with vinaigrettes. First course: this warm tomato tart, a clever riff on the classic Italian caprese salad with a few ingenious twists. Instead of using mozzarella, Dufresne turns soft goat cheese into a tangy sauce. He infuses basil leaves with oil, intensifying their flavor, and caramelizes onions to the height of sweetness to offset the tomatoes' natural acidity. The tart is warmed briefly in the oven, as if by the sun, before it's annointed with swirls of sauce and basil oil. Improving on nature is no easy trick; doing it in under an hour is remarkable. SERVES 6

.INGREDIENTS.

TART
3 large Spanish onions,
    sliced very thin
Salt and freshly ground white pepper
2 tablespoons unsalted butter
Pinch sugar
1 pound puff pastry (if frozen is used,
    2 sheets, partially defrosted)

3 large yellow beefsteak tomatoes
3 large red beefsteak tomatoes
2 tablespoons olive oil
3 tablespoons thinly shredded basil

GOAT CHEESE SAUCE
8 ounces fresh goat cheese
1 cup milk

2 cloves garlic, crushed
1 sprig fresh rosemary
Salt and cayenne

BASIL OIL
1/2 cup plus 1 teaspoon salt
3 cups packed basil leaves
3/4 cup grapeseed oil

1. Preheat the oven to 325º F.

2. TART: Toss the sliced onions with salt and pepper. Melt the butter in a large sauté pan over medium heat. Add the onion and cook, covered, for about 15 minutes. Remove the lid and add a pinch of sugar. Increase the heat and cook until the onions are nicely caramelized, stirring occasionally, about 10 minutes. Remove the onions from the pan and set aside on a plate to cool.

3. Place the puff pastry on a cutting board and, using a 4-inch ring, cut out six disks. Prick the pastry with a fork and place it on a baking tray lined with parchment paper. Place another sheet of parchment paper on the pastry

and an additional baking tray on top to keep the pastry from rising too high. Bake until the pastry turns golden-brown, about 15 to 20 minutes. Remove the top tray and parchment paper and allow the tart shells to cool.

4. Blanch the tomatoes in 4 quarts of boiling water for 15 seconds each, and immediately move them to a large bowl of ice water. Peel, seed, and remove interior ribs from each tomato. Cut the tomatoes into 1/4-inch dice.

5. GOAT CHEESE SAUCE: Crumble the goat cheese into a mixing bowl. Place the milk, garlic, and rosemary in a medium saucepan and bring to a boil. Remove from the heat and allow to sit, covered, for 15 minutes. Reboil the

mixture and strain the milk through a sieve onto the crumbled cheese, whisking until completely smooth. Use additional milk or hot water to thin the sauce if desired. Season to taste with salt and cayenne.

6. BASIL OIL: Bring 2 quarts of water to a boil. Use about ¼ cup salt per quart of hot water. Drop the basil into the boiling water for 15 to 20 seconds, then immediately plunge the basil into ice water to chill. Drain, and squeeze out as much water as possible. Cut the basil into small pieces and place in a blender with oil and salt. Blend on high speed for 2 minutes. Allow to sit for 10 minutes. Strain the purée through a sieve lined with cheesecloth. Discard the cheesecloth and reserve any purée that remains (it can be added to mayonnaise, pasta, or mashed potatoes).

7. Spread the caramelized onions on top of the pastry shells. Mix the red and yellow diced tomatoes together in a bowl, and mound on top of the onions. Season with salt and pepper, then drizzle with olive oil. Bake the tarts for 5 minutes, or until they are warmed through. Place the tarts on six serving plates and garnish the tomatoes with the thinly shredded basil. Drizzle warm goat cheese sauce and basil oil around the tarts and serve.

CLASSIC SWISS FONDUE

FROM TERRANCE BRENNAN *OF* ARTISANAL

How can you not have a good time with a big pot of cheese fondue? That's the way Terrance Brennan sees it. When he was developing the menu for Artisanal, his dairy-dedicated brasserie, he relished the idea of reviving that sixties/seventies-era potluck party staple. At the restaurant, fondue comes a dozen different inventive ways, including an economical "100-cheese" version that uses up assorted odds and ends. Since even a top-of-the-line Subzero is unlikely to have enough shelf space to house that many half-eaten wheels and wedges, we recommend this classic Swiss version, which calls for only Gruyère and Emmentaler. So get out that fondue pot you got as a wedding gift (or borrow your mother's), melt some cheese, and watch those fondue forks fly. NOTE: Encourage guests to make figure eights with their forks as they dip into the fondue and occasionally scrape the bottom of the pot—this motion helps to keep the fondue from separating. If the fondue does separate, return the pot to the stove and whisk hard over medium heat to bring the mixture back together. At the end of the fondue, leave a thin layer of the mixture in the pot over the flame—once it's cool and has caramelized a little, peel off this thin layer and share these last tasty tidbits. It is better to use a heavy ceramic fondue pot for cheese, as it distributes the heat more evenly. SERVES 4

. INGREDIENTS .

1 clove garlic	2 cups shredded Emmental cheese
1 cup dry white wine	2 cups shredded Gruyère cheese
1 tablespoon fresh lemon juice	Pinch freshly grated nutmeg
2 tablespoons Kirschwasser	Sea salt and freshly ground black pepper
1 tablespoon cornstarch	

1. Vigorously rub the garlic clove around the inside of a medium-size heavy-bottomed saucepan. Discard the garlic; add the wine and the lemon juice to the pan and bring to a simmer.

2. In a small bowl, mix the Kirschwasser and the cornstarch until smooth. Add to the saucepan and simmer for 1 minute. Slowly stir in the cheeses until they have melted (the mixture can simmer but not boil). Remove from the heat, stir in the nutmeg, and season to taste with salt and pepper. Transfer to a fondue pot.

3. Serve with assorted cubed breads and your choice of bite-size dippers.

SEARED MARINATED SHRIMP WITH GINGER AND CELERY

FROM BRIAN YOUNG *OF* CITARELLA

In New York, the name "Citarella" is synonymous with seafood. First came the rapidly expanding chain of gourmet fish shops stretching from the Upper West Side to the Hamptons and then the elegant seafood restaurant in Rockefeller Center. So when we were searching for something spectacular to do with pristinely fresh shrimp for our casual cocktail party issue, we instantly thought of Brian Young, chef at Citarella at the time. Before he marinates the shrimp in a piquant mixture of crushed ginger, celery leaves, scallions, cilantro, and mint, he sears them, locking in their subtle natural flavor. After four hours, they emerge triumphant, with a remarkably unrubbery texture and so well seasoned they don't need a dip. YIELDS 24 PIECES

. INGREDIENTS .

4 ounces fresh ginger, peeled, cut into large chunks
3 stalks celery with leaves
3 scallions
Large bunch fresh cilantro
Large bunch fresh mint
¼ cup mirin

2 tablespoons hot sesame oil (Asian sesame oil mixed with ¼ teaspoon cayenne may be substituted)
24 shrimp (15-20 size), peeled and deveined
Salt and finely ground black pepper
Canola oil for sautéing

1. Place the ginger, celery, scallions, cilantro, and mint on a large cutting board and pound with the bottom of a heavy saucepan until smashed. Place in a large bowl and add the mirin and sesame oil.

2. Season the shrimp with salt and pepper. Heat a few drops of canola oil in a nonstick sauté pan over medium-high heat. Add the shrimp in batches and sear for 2 minutes per side, until just opaque. Immediately add the shrimp to the marinade and toss to coat. (There will be very little liquid in the bowl at this stage.) Allow to cool, and marinate in the refrigerator for 2 to 4 hours, tossing the shrimp once or twice. Serve the shrimp mounded on a platter.

DEVILED EGGS

FROM **MICHAEL ROMANO** *AND*
KENNY CALLAGHAN *OF* **BLUE SMOKE**

When restaurateur Danny Meyer opened his barbecue joint, Blue Smoke, he knew he wanted a menu that was simpler and folksier than at his four other, more upscale restaurants. He relied on Michael Romano, the chef at his Union Square Cafe, to collaborate with Blue Smoke chef Kenny Callaghan on just the right delicious down-home formula. They've succeeded, as nightly crowds attest, and it's more than the Memphis-style ribs that draw them in. The deviled eggs appetizer is a perfect example of a classic with character. The yolks are seasoned with Dijon and Coleman's dry mustards and a touch of curry spice and then piped into their whites. Simple. If you're smart, you'll make a lot. I find that whenever I serve them, they're the first hors d'oeuvre to disappear, no matter how jaded my guests' palates. NOTE: Make sure to follow the cooking instructions for the eggs to avoid discoloration around the egg yolk. YIELDS 24 PIECES

. INGREDIENTS .

12 large eggs
²/₃ cup mayonnaise
1½ teaspoons tarragon-infused
    champagne vinegar
¾ teaspoon Colman's dry mustard

2½ teaspoons Dijon mustard
⅓ teaspoon cayenne
½ teaspoon curry powder
Salt and freshly ground black pepper
Sweet paprika, for garnish

1. Place the eggs in a saucepan, cover with cold water, and bring to a boil over high heat. Reduce the heat and simmer for exactly 9 minutes. Pour off most of the water and immediately run cold water over the eggs.

2. Crack the eggshells and peel the eggs under running water. Cut a small sliver off both ends of each egg and halve them crosswise, forming round cups. Remove the yolks and reserve. Pass the yolks through a fine sieve into a bowl. Add the mayonnaise, vinegar, mustards,

cayenne, and curry powder to the bowl, and mix together with a rubber spatula until smooth. Season to taste with salt and pepper.

3. Spoon the egg-yolk paste into a pastry bag with a star tip, and pipe the mixture into the egg whites to form rosettes. (Or use a teaspoon to mound the yolk into the egg whites.) Sprinkle the top of the eggs with paprika. Refrigerate immediately.

CLASSIC TERRINE OF FOIE GRAS

FROM ARIANE DAGUIN *OF* D'ARTAGNAN ROTISSERIE

If there was ever a moment to splurge on big-ticket items like caviar, truffles, and foie gras, the millennium was it. At the time, gastronomic excess—and our expense accounts—seemed to know no bounds. To procure the best recipe for foie gras terrine, we went to the source (or as close as we could get without actually trespassing on a goose farm). We called Ariane Daguin, second-generation Gascon restaurateur and purveyor of game meats and foie gras to America's most discriminating palates. At D'Artagnan, her rustic rotisserie restaurant, foie gras is almost a religion; devout followers take communion in the adorable form of French Kisses, Armagnac-soaked prunes stuffed with foie gras. Daguin's terrine recipe is gratifyingly simple: Immerse a whole liver in Sauternes and cook it slowly at a very low temperature. Chill, slice, sprinkle with fleur de sel, and serve with crusty peasant bread and a glass of Sauternes. At about $62 for a whole Grade A French foie gras, this might not be the most economical dish, but think of something to celebrate—sensations this voluptuous shouldn't come only once a millennium. SERVES 8 TO 10

. INGREDIENTS .

1 whole Grade A French foie gras, about 1¼ pounds	Salt and freshly ground white pepper ⅔ cup Sauternes

1. Preheat the oven to 200° F.

2. Allow the foie gras to come to room temperature for about 30 minutes, so it doesn't crack. Place the smooth side of the foie gras down on a cutting board, with the smaller lobe to your right. Pull the two lobes apart. With the larger lobe lying smooth-side down, gently pull away the surface membrane. Peel back the flesh of the liver to expose the central vein, which runs about three-quarters of the way down the middle of the large lobe before it branches. Gently pull out as many of the small veins that are attached as possible, holding the foie gras down with your other hand so you don't break the liver. With a small paring knife, remove any green flesh, bloody spots, or other imperfections, and discard the membranes and veins. Repeat with the smaller lobe.

3. Season the liver generously with salt and pepper. Place the large lobe smooth-side down in a rectangular or oval porcelain terrine mold about the same size as the foie gras. Pour a little of the Sauternes over it. Add any broken pieces of the liver, a little more Sauternes, and finally the smaller lobe, smooth-side up, sprinkled with the rest of the wine. Cover the terrine with its lid or with microwavable plastic wrap.

4. Put a folded kitchen towel or six paper towels layered together in the bottom of a pan large enough to hold the terrine, and set the terrine on top. Fill the pan halfway up the sides of the terrine with hot (not boiling) water, and bake until the internal temperature measures 120° F on an instant-read thermometer (about 1 hour, depending on the thickness of the terrine).

5. Remove the terrine from the water bath and place it in a dish. Invert the lid to exert a light pressure on the liver. This will force enough fat to the surface to cover the liver, and some may spill over the side. (If the terrine does not have a lid, or if the lid has a protruding handle, cut a piece of cardboard slightly smaller than the top of the mold and encase it in several layers of plastic wrap.) Place the inverted lid (or cardboard) on the liver and weigh it down (two 1-pound cans from your pantry work well) for 1½ hours at room temperature. Then remove the weights and cover the liver with any fat that spilled into the outer dish.

6. When the foie gras is entirely covered by its fat, wrap the terrine tightly and refrigerate for at least 3 days before serving. (It will keep for 2 weeks.)

7. To serve, unmold by dipping the terrine briefly in hot water and inverting. Using a hot knife, cut into serving slices. Serve slices sprinkled with a pinch of fleur de sel (sea salt), slices of peasant bread, and a glass of Sauternes.

2
SOUPS
AND
SALADS

Madison Chopped Salad (page 49)

BORSCHT

FROM SERENA BASS *OF* SERENA BASS CATERING *AND* SERENA

When it comes to entertaining, Serena Bass is a professional. While she's running her catering company and Serena, the trendy bar she opened with her son in the basement of Manhattan's fabled Chelsea Hotel, she's all business, but entertaining friends and family at her Connecticut country house is pure pleasure. To keep it that way, Bass sticks to dishes she can cook ahead of time, like this exquisitely seasoned borscht. The secret ingredient is Aleppo pepper, an unexpected flavor that makes as much of an impact as the savory soup's telltale magenta hue. NOTE: The borscht can be served hot or cold. SERVES 8

. INGREDIENTS .

3 pounds medium beets, unpeeled (about
    12 medium beets)

2 tablespoons vegetable oil

2 large onions, coarsely chopped

1/2 small white cabbage, shredded
    (about 8 ounces)

4 cloves garlic

12 cups chicken stock

4 whole cloves

2 bay leaves

1 tablespoon Aleppo pepper (1 teaspoon
    red-pepper flakes can be substituted)

2 tablespoons whole black peppercorns

1 Knorr beef bouillon cube

Sea salt

1/2 cup sour cream

2 tablespoons sherry vinegar

1/2 cup crème fraîche

1/2 cup chopped fresh dill

1. Preheat the oven to 350º F.

2. Cut half of the beets into 1-inch pieces. Heat the oil in a large, heavy-bottomed stockpot; add the beets, onion, cabbage, and garlic, and sauté until the onion is translucent. Add the chicken stock, cloves, bay leaves, Aleppo pepper, black peppercorns, and bouillon cube. Cover the stockpot, bring to a boil, and simmer for 1 1/4 hours. Simmer until you have about 7 cups.

3. Place the remaining beets in a glass dish. Add 1/4 inch of water and cover with foil. Roast in the oven for about 1 hour, or until the beets are cooked. When they're cool, peel and roughly dice.

4. Strain the beet-cabbage mixture, discarding the solids. Add the liquid to a blender with the reserved roasted diced beets and sour cream, in batches, and purée until smooth. Add the sherry vinegar, and season to taste with salt. Place in the refrigerator until well chilled. Serve chilled in individual bowls, each topped with a swirl of crème fraîche and garnished with dill.

SENEGALESE PEANUT SOUP

FROM LESLIE KAUL *OF* DAILY SOUP

Takeout soup was such an improbable hit by 1996 that you never knew who might turn up stirring the pot and ladling out the stuff at one of the city's burgeoning soup shops, kiosks, and kitchens. Leslie Kaul, who did time at Lespinasse, Union Square Cafe, and Gramercy Tavern, three of New York's top restaurants, was so soup-smitten she enlisted in Daily Soup, a soon-to-be chain of minimalist, cafeteria-style takeout shops, where she introduced a repertoire of about 500 soups, ten to fourteen of which were available daily. This soup's smooth texture contrasts nicely with the crunchy peanuts, and curry gives it a sweet-and-spicy effect. Serve it with a crusty peasant loaf, and you have a satisfying vegetarian-friendly winter meal. SERVES 6 TO 8

. INGREDIENTS .

2 tablespoons peanut oil

1 red onion, diced

3 stalks celery, diced

2 leeks, roughly chopped

4 cloves garlic, sliced thin

$1/2$–$3/4$ teaspoon cayenne, to taste

2 teaspoons curry powder

1 teaspoon ground cumin

1 teaspoon ground coriander

4 beefsteak tomatoes, seeded, roughly chopped

2 cups salted roasted peanuts, plus $1/4$ cup for garnish

4 cups vegetable stock

1 tablespoon sugar

$1/2$ cup heavy cream

Pinch kosher salt

$1/4$ cup chopped fresh chives

1. Heat the oil in a soup pot. Sweat the onion, celery, leeks, and garlic until soft.

2. Add the cayenne, curry, cumin, and coriander and cook for 3 to 5 minutes. Add three-quarters of the tomato and 1 cup of peanuts; cook for 5 minutes. Add the vegetable stock, bring to a boil, and simmer, covered, for 20 minutes. Purée the sugar, remaining 1 cup of peanuts, and the remaining tomato in a food processor. Add this paste to the soup, and cook for another 5 minutes. Add the cream and bring the soup to a boil. Remove from the heat, season to taste with salt, and garnish with chives and chopped peanuts.

SWEET CORN-AND- LOBSTER CHOWDER

FROM JEREMY MARSHALL *OF* AQUAGRILL

Nothing says summer like fresh sweet corn, except maybe lobster. Celebrate the season to the fullest, then, by combining the two in this delightful all-American chowder. The recipe comes from Jeremy Marshall, the chef and co-owner of Aquagrill, a quiet little gem of a SoHo seafood restaurant. Simmering the lobsters (and later their shells) with the cobs achieves an intensely flavored broth. The fresh corn kernels are then briefly simmered separately in the broth before they're puréed and poured over the succulent lobster meat. A drizzle of jalapeño-scallion oil adds an exotic touch. SERVES 4

. INGREDIENTS .

Two 1-pound lobsters
8 ears of corn
2 small onions
2 stalks celery
3 tablespoons canola oil
4 cloves garlic, smashed
4 sprigs fresh cilantro, plus 1 teaspoon,
   chopped, for garnish
1 1/2 teaspoons salt

2 quarts chicken stock
2 tablespoons unsalted butter
1/4 teaspoon freshly ground white pepper
Jalapeño-Scallion Oil (recipe follows)

JALAPEÑO-SCALLION OIL
3 scallions, cut into 2-inch pieces
1/2 jalapeño pepper, including seeds
1/4 teaspoon salt
1 cup canola oil

1. Place the lobster, hard shell facing up, on a cutting board. Just behind the head, there is a cross mark in the shell. Plunge a large knife through the mark all the way to the cutting board, and draw the knife straight down toward the eyes (approximately 1 inch). When the lobster stops moving, it's dead. Wash the lobsters well to remove sand.

2. Cut the corn kernels from the cobs and reserve both the kernels and cobs. Cut onions and celery into 1-inch pieces. Heat the canola oil in a heavy 10-quart pot until just smoking. Add the lobsters and sauté carefully for 1 minute on each side. Add the onion, celery, garlic, cobs, cilantro sprigs, and 1 teaspoon of salt. Sauté for 2 minutes. Add 4 cups of water and the stock. Cover and bring to a boil. Remove the lobsters as soon as the liquid begins to boil. Set the lobsters aside to cool on a tray, and remove the meat from the claws and tail once

they're cool enough to handle. Dice the lobster meat into large chunks and cover with a damp towel. Return the shells to the pot and continue to simmer the stock for an additional 45 minutes. Strain through a colander and reserve the liquid.

3. Melt the butter in a large saucepan and add the kernels. Season with the remaining 1/2 teaspoon salt and the white pepper. Sauté for 2 minutes over medium heat. Add 6 cups of the reserved liquid and simmer for 10 minutes. Remove from the heat and purée in a blender until coarse. Adjust the seasoning. Pour the chowder over the lobster in soup bowls that have been warmed in the oven. Drizzle spicy oil on top and garnish with chopped cilantro.

4. JALAPEÑO-SCALLION OIL: Purée all of the ingredients in a blender until smooth. Set aside for at least an hour.

TUNA-SASHIMI SALAD

FROM NOBU MATSUHISA *OF* NOBU

When Robert De Niro finally persuaded Nobu Matsuhisa to open an East Coast bra
was an instant hit. And thanks to the chef's innovative nouvelle-Peruvian take on
still is. You'll have better luck making this deceptively simple salad yourself than
signal on the reservations line, especially if you start, as Nobu insists you must, with it
tuna, preferably from a Japanese market where it's precut into blocks for sashimi. T
quickly searing the fish and plunging it into icy water to stop the cooking. The entre
famous Matsuhisa dressing, but it's just as easy to make your own. SERVES 6

. INGREDIENTS .

1 medium-size onion, finely chopped	Salt and freshly ground blac
1 cup soy sauce	1 pound tuna (very fresh; lo
½ cup vegetable oil	color, avoiding brown-bla
½ cup sesame oil	saggy flesh)
½ cup rice vinegar	6 handfuls mesclun
2 tablespoons sugar	

1. Combine the onion, soy sauce, oils, vinegar, and sugar with 6 tablespoons of water in a bowl. Add salt and pepper to taste. Set aside for 2 hours.

2. Trim the tuna to a block 1 inch deep by 1 ¾ inches wide by 5 inches long. (You can find fish already cut into blocks for sashimi at most Japanese markets.) Season with salt

and pepper. Heat a grill until very hot and just sear the tuna on all sides. Plunge the tuna briefly into cold water. When it's cool, cut it into thin slices on the bias.

3. Place a mound of mesclun on a plate and arrange the tuna slices around the salad. Stir the dressing and pour around the tuna and the perimeter of the plate.

MADISON CHOPPED SALAD

FROM MARK STRAUSMAN *OF* CAMPAGNA

Before Mark Strausman opened Campagna, he was the chef at Coco Pazzo on Manhattan's Upper East Side, where he became adept at fielding special requests from what might be the world's most finicky clientele. This salad, which became a Strausman signature, was born in that demanding atmosphere as a concession to calorie-counting diners who couldn't be bothered to struggle with unwieldy lettuce leaves. An Italian take on the classic Cobb, it mixes beans, greens, and a long farmers'-market shopping list of crunchy vegetables with canned tuna and shaved Parmesan for a chopped salad that eats like a meal. It's a great clean-out-your-fridge recipe: Use whatever you have on hand, as long as the textures vary. SERVES 4

.INGREDIENTS.

8 ounces mesclun
1 bunch arugula
1 Belgian endive
1/2 head radicchio
One 12-ounce can water-packed tuna, drained
1 cup shaved Parmesan cheese (about 3 ounces)
1/2 cup finely chopped tomatoes, seeded
1/2 cup finely minced red onion
1/2 cup cooked peas
1/2 cup chopped cooked asparagus
2 large white button mushrooms, very thinly sliced
1/4 cup diced red bell pepper
1/4 cup diced yellow bell pepper

1/4 cup cooked lentils
1/4 cup cooked Great Northern beans
1/4 cup diced cooked beets
1/4 cup chopped cooked green beans
1/2 cup diced cooked potatoes
1/4 cup chopped scallion
1/4 cup diced raw zucchini
Vinaigrette (recipe follows)

VINAIGRETTE
1 large clove garlic, crushed
1/4 cup red wine vinegar
3/4 cup extra-virgin olive oil
Salt and freshly ground black pepper to taste

1. Finely chop the mesclun, arugula, endive, and radicchio. Place in a large salad bowl. Add the remaining ingredients and toss together well. Stir in the vinaigrette and mix lightly until everything is coated.

2. VINAIGRETTE: Place the garlic in a stainless-steel bowl and add the vinegar. Set aside for an hour, then add the olive oil, salt, and pepper. Whisk well.

GRILLED SEA-SCALLOP SALAD WITH RED-PEPPER CONSERVE

FROM MARK SPANGENTHAL *OF* THE MARKHAM

At the critically acclaimed (if short-lived) Markham, chef Mark Spangenthal's straightforward American cooking made optimal use of seasonal ingredients like the ones that animate this grilled sea-scallop salad. Actually, it's three salads in one: a bed of peppery arugula, a ring of oil-and-vinegar-slicked new potatoes, and a pepper-flecked mound of grilled sweet corn—a lively show of summery support for succulent scallops drizzled with piquant red-pepper conserve. NOTE: The scallops and corn can be grilled on a cast-iron grill if you don't have a barbecue handy. SERVES 4

. INGREDIENTS .

4 ears corn, shucked

6 tablespoons extra-virgin olive oil plus extra for brushing corn and scallops

Salt and freshly ground black pepper

4 red bell peppers, diced

3 shallots, minced

2 cloves garlic, minced

1 tablespoon minced fresh chives

3 teaspoons fresh lemon juice

Pinch cayenne

8 new potatoes

1 tablespoon chopped fresh parsley

1 teaspoon red wine vinegar

12 to 16 large sea scallops

2 bunches arugula, stems removed

1. Blanch the corn for a least 4 minutes in a large pot of salted boiling water. Remove the corn from the water, brush with olive oil, and season with salt and pepper. Light a charcoal grill. Grill corn until golden brown. Allow the corn to cool, then cut the kernels from the cob. In a bowl, mix the corn with one-quarter of the diced pepper, two-thirds of the shallots, half the garlic, the chives, 2 tablespoons of olive oil, and 1 teaspoon of lemon juice. Season to taste.

2. Place the remaining red pepper and garlic in a saucepan with 2 tablespoons of olive oil, the cayenne, 2 teaspoons of lemon juice, and 2 cups of water. Bring to a boil, then simmer until almost all the water has evaporated. Set aside.

3. In a saucepan, boil the potatoes until tender. Drain and allow to cool. Slice the potatoes into rounds, place in a bowl, and add the remaining shallot, the parsley, 2 table-spoons of olive oil, and the vinegar. Stir gently and set aside.

4. Brush the scallops with olive oil, season with salt and pepper, and grill for 4 minutes on each side. Arrange some arugula on each plate. Place the corn salad in the middle and surround the corn with the potato salad. Position the scallops atop the corn salad and garnish with red-pepper conserve.

3
PASTA

Spaghetti in Cartocchio (Baked in a Pouch with Seafood) (page 61)

CAVATELLI WITH OVEN-ROASTED EGGPLANT, TOMATOES, BASIL, AND RICOTTA SALATA

FROM LIDIA BASTIANICH *OF* FELIDIA

No matter how hectic her schedule, Lidia Bastianich—savvy restaurateur, beloved television personality, acclaimed cookbook author, and flat-out awesome cook—still finds time to gather her extended family around her table in Douglaston, Queens, for Sunday lunch. Since her waterside property teems with fig trees, grape arbors, and a bountiful vegetable garden, and her cellar is crammed with homemade prosciutto, salami, pancetta, and vinegar, Lidia seldom has to leave the grounds to buy ingredients. Lunch is a collaborative affair: Her son selects the wine, her mother collects eggplant and tomatoes from the garden, and Lidia roasts them to intensify their just-picked flavor. Then she tosses them with pasta, ricotta salata, and freshly snipped basil for proof positive that the best food has the shortest trip from plot to pot. SERVES 8

· INGREDIENTS ·

1 cup freshly made bread crumbs (preferably from two-day-old country bread, ground in a food processor)
2 teaspoons chopped fresh thyme
Pinch crushed red-pepper flakes
1 cup grated Pecorino Romano
1/2 cup extra-virgin olive oil
4 cups red and yellow cherry tomatoes

Salt
2 medium eggplants, cut into 1/2-inch-thick slices
6 garlic cloves, sliced
1 cup chicken stock
1 1/2 pounds dried cavatelli or cavatappi
1/4 cup chopped fresh basil
2 ounces ricotta salata

1. Preheat the oven to 425º F.

2. Toss the bread crumbs, thyme, crushed red-pepper flakes, 2 tablespoons of Pecorino Romano, and 2 tablespoons of oil in a bowl. Place the cherry tomatoes in a single layer on a baking pan, drizzle with 1 tablespoon of the oil, and season to taste with salt. Toss until the tomatoes are covered with oil. Sprinkle the seasoned bread crumbs over the tomatoes, and bake in the oven for about 7 minutes, or until the tomatoes start to crack and the bread crumbs are crisp and toasted.

3. Lay the eggplant slices on an oiled baking sheet, brush them with 2 tablespoons of oil, and salt them to taste. Bake in the oven for 10 minutes, turning them once when they're golden on one side. Remove and set aside. When they're cool, cut them into 1-inch cubes.

4. In the meantime, bring 8 quarts of salted water to a boil. Heat the remaining oil in a large skillet, add the garlic, and sauté until golden. Add the chicken stock (be careful—it may splatter) and bring to a vigorous boil; add salt to taste and a pinch of crushed red-pepper flakes.

5. Cook the pasta for 5 to 7 minutes, until al dente. Drain the pasta, add to the skillet, and sauté with the garlic. Add the tomatoes, bread crumbs (do not add the crumbs sticking to the pan if they are burnt or mushy), and eggplant, toss together gently, then quickly stir in the remaining Pecorino Romano and basil. Serve with freshly grated ricotta salata on top.

DAD'S MACARONI AND CHEESE

FROM DAVID PAGE *OF* HOME

Long before macaroni and cheese was trendy, David Page was nurturing a comfort food-starved crowd at his cozy West Village restaurant, Home. Page cooks the type of honest, wholesome, unabashedly all-American dishes that you might recall from your own childhood, had that childhood taken place on a Midwestern farm, say, and had your mother been the kind of talented down-home cook who made her own ketchup. Like many of his recipes, this one is rooted in his Wisconsin childhood. Thursday night *chez* Page was Dad's turn to cook, and Dad's specialty was skillet macaroni and cheese. David, like Dad, recommends a combination of high-quality, freshly grated Cheddar, Wisconsin Asiago, and dry Jack. He tops the dish with sliced tomato and bread crumbs for an exceptionally crunchy crust and bakes it in a cast-iron skillet. SERVES 6 TO 8

. INGREDIENTS .

4 tablespoons (½ stick) unsalted butter, plus extra for the skillet

1 large yellow onion, cut into ⅛-inch dice

1 tablespoon minced garlic

3 tablespoons all-purpose flour

4 cups whole milk

1 teaspoon paprika

½ teaspoon ground nutmeg

2 teaspoons kosher salt

1 teaspoon freshly ground black pepper

¾ cup grated extra-sharp Cheddar cheese

¾ cup grated Wisconsin Asiago cheese

¾ cup grated dry Jack cheese (Parmesan can be substituted)

1 pound elbow macaroni, cooked and drained

2 plum tomatoes, sliced

½ cup fresh bread crumbs

1 tablespoon chopped fresh parsley

1 tablespoon chopped fresh thyme

1 tablespoon chopped fresh chives

1. Preheat the oven to 400° F.

2. Melt the butter in a large pot over medium heat. Add the onion and garlic, and cook until they are softened, about 2 minutes. Whisk in the flour and cook, stirring constantly, until the mixture turns light brown, about 3 minutes. Gradually whisk in the milk. Add the paprika, nutmeg, salt, and pepper. Reduce the heat to low and cook, stirring, until the sauce is thickened, about 5 minutes. Add the cheeses and stir until they are melted. Add the macaroni and stir until the noodles are thoroughly coated. Remove from the heat. (Do not allow the macaroni to sit at this stage, as it will dry out.)

3. Butter two 6-inch cast-iron skillets or one 12-inch skillet. Transfer the macaroni mixture to the skillets. Top with the sliced tomatoes. Sprinkle bread crumbs on top. Bake until the cheese is bubbling and golden-brown, about 30 minutes. Garnish with the chopped herbs.

LASAGNA BOLOGNESE

FROM MARIO BATALI *OF* BABBO

Late in the fall of 2001, New Yorkers were craving comfort food and the companionship of loved ones. Our 2001 holiday entertaining issue reflected that trend, incorporating homey recipes from top chefs like "Molto" Mario Batali, who grew up in an Italian-American family that spent weekends cooking and eating together. Now, when he's not behind one of his four ranges or on a cooking-show set, he continues that Sunday-afternoon tradition with his own two boys. His luscious lasagna bolognese, based on a recipe he learned as a young cook in Emilia-Romagna, might take some time to assemble, but when everyone's involved, it's time well spent. On its own his ragù, a deeply flavored mixture of veal, pork, and pancetta, would ennoble a bowl of spaghetti, but here, it marries sublimely with the creamy, nutty béchamel. And best of all, what seems to be a laborious task is actually a timesaver: The lasagna can be made a day or two ahead, or even frozen. SERVES 6 TO 8

. INGREDIENTS .

RAGÙ
¼ cup extra-virgin olive oil
2 medium onions, finely chopped
1 carrot, finely chopped
4 stalks celery, finely chopped

5 cloves garlic, sliced
1 pound veal, ground
1 pound pork, ground
4 ounces pancetta, ground
One 8-ounce can tomato paste

1 cup milk
½ cup white wine
1 teaspoon fresh thyme leaves
Salt and freshly ground
    black pepper

BÉCHAMEL
5 tablespoons unsalted butter
¼ cup all-purpose flour
3 cups milk
2 teaspoons salt or to taste
½ teaspoon freshly grated nutmeg

LASAGNA
Melted butter or olive oil for brushing
¾ to 1 pound fresh pasta sheets, about 7 x 4 inches,
    or dried lasagna noodles blanched for
    6 minutes and refreshed in ice water
1 cup freshly grated Parmigiano-Reggiano

1. RAGÙ: In a large heavy-bottomed saucepan, heat the olive oil. Add the onion, carrot, celery, and garlic, and sweat over medium heat for about 5 minutes, until the vegetables are translucent. Add the veal, pork, and pancetta to the vegetables, and brown over high heat, stirring to keep the meat from sticking together. Add the tomato paste, milk, wine, thyme, and 1 cup of water, and simmer over medium-low heat for 1 to 1½ hours (if the ragù becomes too thick, add a little more water). Season to taste with salt and pepper and remove from the heat.

2. BÉCHAMEL: Melt the butter in a medium saucepan, add the flour, and whisk until smooth. Cook over medium heat, stirring regularly, until the mixture turns golden-brown, about 6 to 7 minutes.

3. Meanwhile, heat the milk in a separate pan until it is just about to boil. Add the milk to the butter mixture, 1 cup at a time, whisking continuously until the sauce is very smooth. Bring to a boil and cook for 30 seconds longer. Remove from the heat and season with salt and nutmeg.

4. ASSEMBLY: Preheat the oven to 375º F.

5. Brush a 9 x 13-inch glass baking dish with melted butter or oil, and layer in the following order from the bottom: ragù, pasta, béchamel, and grated cheese (saving about 1 cup of béchamel for the last topping), making three to four layers of pasta, finishing with ragù, béchamel, and ¼ cup of the Parmigiano-Reggiano sprinkled over the top. Bake in the oven for 45 minutes, until the top is golden brown and the casserole is bubbling. Remove from the oven, allow to cool for 20 minutes, slice, and serve.

Stuffed and Roasted Wild Striped Bass (page 66)

STUFFED AND ROASTED WILD STRIPED BASS

FROM MICHAEL LOMONACO *OF* WILD BLUE

Michael Lomonaco's full-flavored, seasonally inspired American cooking made Wild Blue at Windows on the World a foodie destination. This whole roasted wild striped bass is indicative of his rustic, satisfying style, and he recommended it as a turkey alternative for one of our Thanksgiving-themed issues. Wrapped with string and stuffed with vegetables and bread crumbs, it makes a dramatic presentation that works equally well at a holiday banquet or a low-key dinner party. NOTE: Salmon can be substituted for the striped bass. SERVES 8

·INGREDIENTS·

½ cup olive oil

3 small white onions, diced

1 pound fresh whole leeks,
 white part only diced and washed

½ pound carrots, peeled and thinly sliced into rounds

Sea salt and freshly ground black pepper

1 cup drained canned plum tomatoes, coarsely chopped

3 cups chopped spinach leaves

½ cup dry white wine

3 tablespoons chopped garlic

2 tablespoons fresh thyme leaves

2 tablespoons fresh chopped tarragon leaves

½ pound day-old French bread, cut into ½-inch
 cubes and soaked in ½ cup milk

One 6- to 7-pound wild striped bass, scales removed,
 gutted, butterflied, head on or off

1. Heat 2 tablespoons of the oil in a large skillet over medium heat for 1 minute. Add the onion, leek, and carrot, and season with salt and pepper. Cook until wilted, about 7 to 9 minutes. Add the tomatoes, and stir to combine. Cook for several minutes to allow any excess juice to cook off before removing the vegetables with a slotted spoon to a platter. Add 2 more tablespoons of the oil to the skillet and heat for a moment; then add the spinach leaves. Cook for 2 to 3 minutes, until the spinach has wilted, drain any excess liquid, and return the cooked vegetables and wine to the pan. Stir to combine well and cook for 1 minute. Add the garlic, thyme, and tarragon; cook for 2 minutes and stir in the moistened bread. Season to taste with salt and pepper, and remove the skillet from the heat. Transfer the stuffing to a cookie sheet and chill in the refrigerator.

2. Preheat the oven to 425° F.

3. Select a roasting pan large enough to hold the bass lengthwise, and drizzle 3 tablespoons of oil over the bottom of the pan. Place the bass on the pan, spread open the cavity, and season the fish with salt and pepper. Fill the body of the fish with the chilled vegetable stuffing, spreading it evenly. Close the fish, sandwiching the stuffing inside, rub the remaining oil over the skin of the bass, and season with salt and pepper. Tie the fish with string at intervals to seal the stuffing inside.

4. Place the roasting pan in the oven and roast for 45 to 60 minutes, or until the fish is firm and the stuffing in the center is thoroughly hot (the center of the fish should read 140° F on an instant-read thermometer). Remove from the oven and allow to rest for 20 minutes before serving, or let cool and serve at room temperature.

PROVENÇAL FISH STEW

FROM DAVID WALTUCK *OF* CHANTERELLE

One of our entertaining issues explored what top chefs cook at home, with predictably delicious and surprisingly simple results. This wonderful recipe came from Chanterelle chef-owner David Waltuck. Chanterelle is a formal restaurant, a special-occasion type of place, but when David entertains at home with his wife, Karen, he prefers casual dishes that let him relax with his guests. This spectacular fish stew, akin to bouillabaisse and heady with a Provençal perfume, is one of them. The saffron-scented, Pernod-spiked broth can be made in advance and refrigerated or frozen. Lobster, monkfish, shrimp, and clams are poached in the broth just before serving, and slices of freshly toasted bread spread with a garlicky aïoli float on the surface. Consider it the professional chef's version of how to win friends and influence people without really trying. NOTE: This broth can be used for poaching whatever fish and/or shellfish are desired. SERVES 6

·INGREDIENTS·

½ cup virgin olive oil	Salt
1 large onion, coarsely chopped	Juice of ½ lemon
2 carrots, coarsely chopped	One 1-pound lobster (optional)
1 fennel bulb, coarsely chopped	1 ½ pounds monkfish or halibut fillets,
2 garlic bulbs, unpeeled, coarsely chopped	skinned and cut into 1-inch chunks
1 cup white wine	12 shrimp, shelled and deveined
¼ cup Pernod	12 sea scallops
1 cup canned tomatoes, crushed	24 mussels and/or clams, soaked in cold water
Saffron	for 1 hour and cleaned
1 quart fish stock	18 toasted baguette rounds
Three 2-inch long pieces orange zest	¾ cup aïoli (mayonnaise flavored strongly
2 bay leaves	with crushed garlic)

1. Heat the olive oil and sweat the onion, carrot, fennel, and garlic in a covered skillet set over low heat. When softened but not browned, add the wine and Pernod, and reduce by half. Add the tomatoes, a very large pinch of saffron, the fish stock, orange zest, and bay leaves. Simmer for 30 minutes.

2. Strain, and discard the vegetables; boil the liquid to reduce it slightly. Season to taste with salt, lemon juice, and more Pernod and saffron, if necessary.

3. Add the lobster (if desired) to the simmering broth, and cook for 5 minutes. Add the fish chunks, and cook for 3 minutes longer. Add the shrimp, scallops, and mussels or clams, and cook until the shells open, about 2 to 3 minutes longer. Break off the lobster claws and discard the head.

4. Ladle the broth and seafood into bowls, and serve with toasted baguette rounds spread with aïoli.

Roast Duck à l'Orange (page 92)

ROASTED CHICKEN

FROM SCOTT BRYAN *OF* VERITAS

Everyone knows how to roast a chicken, but few do it as well as Scott Bryan, whose refined New American menu at Veritas complements one of New York's longest and most exciting wine lists. A bit too rustic for his finely tuned restaurant kitchen, this version is exactly the sort of food Bryan likes to cook at home. He starts by rubbing an organic chicken with lemon and butter. Then he stuffs the cavity with sprigs of thyme, rosemary, and tarragon and sets the bird on a bed of vegetables, which soak up the herb-scented juices as they cook. After an hour the skin is crisp, the meat is tender, and the vegetables are perfectly roasted. It's one-pot cooking at its tantalizing best. SERVES 6 TO 8

. INGREDIENTS .

1 to 1 ½ pounds fingerling potatoes, washed and halved

2 large carrots, peeled and cut into 1-inch pieces

2 large parsnips, peeled and cut into 1-inch pieces

10 shallots, peeled and halved

15 cremini mushrooms, halved

5 garlic cloves, peeled

3 tablespoons extra-virgin olive oil

Salt and freshly ground black pepper

1 lemon

Two 3½-pound organic chickens

4 tablespoons (½ stick) unsalted butter, at room temperature

4 sprigs each fresh tarragon, rosemary, and thyme

1 cup dry white wine

Fleur de sel (sea salt)

1. Preheat the oven to 425° F.

2. Toss the potatoes, carrots, parsnips, shallots, mushrooms, and garlic with the oil and a generous pinch of salt and pepper in a large roasting pan. Cut the lemon in half, and rub the chickens with the lemon flesh and then the butter; season the birds generously with salt and pepper. Place half a lemon and two sprigs each of tarragon, rosemary, and thyme in the cavity of each chicken.

3. Arrange the chickens on top of the vegetables, and roast in the lower half of the oven for 45 minutes to 1 hour, or until the chickens are cooked and the skin is crisp, basting the chickens every 20 minutes. If the birds are not crisp, increase the oven temperature to 475° F for the last 10 to 15 minutes of cooking.

4. Remove from the oven, cover the chickens loosely with aluminum foil, and allow the chickens and vegetables to rest in the pan for 20 minutes.

5. Remove the chicken and vegetables to a platter, pour the fat off the pan, deglaze with the wine, and season to taste with salt and pepper. Sprinkle the carved chicken and vegetables with fleur de sel, and serve with pan juices.

CHICKEN BREASTS WITH CAPERS, OLIVES, AND ANCHOVIES

FROM UMBERTO ASSANTE *OF* DA UMBERTO

Umberto Assante opened his Tuscan restaurant Da Umberto in Chelsea in the late eighties. His style of entertaining friends at home, like the atmosphere at Da Umberto, is true Tuscan: simple and casual, featuring his healthy, tasty Italian dishes. Assante's recipe for sautéed chicken breasts showered with a confetti of red peppers, capers, and olives is one of his favorites. As it can be cooked in half an hour, it makes a terrific quick summer lunch or dinner that's simply bursting with vibrant Mediterranean flavors. NOTE: Even the anchovy-averse shouldn't be put off by the fact that the recipe calls for the tiny fish, since they're used sparingly and cooked down into the sauce to give it a wonderful depth of flavor, without giving it a too distinctive anchovy taste.

SERVES 6

·INGREDIENTS·

6 large boneless, skinless chicken breast halves
Flour for dredging
$1/2$ cup vegetable oil
$1/4$ cup olive oil
24 gaeta olives
$1/2$ red bell pepper, julienned
3 tablespoons capers

$1/4$ cup white wine
4 anchovies, drained and chopped
Salt and freshly ground black pepper
2 tablespoons chopped fresh parsley
1 tablespoon chopped fresh basil
$1/2$ cup chicken stock

1. Dredge the chicken breasts in flour. Heat the vegetable oil in a large skillet; add the chicken and brown quickly on both sides. Remove from the pan, and discard the oil.

2. Heat the olive oil in the skillet, add the chicken, olives, red pepper, and capers, and simmer briefly. Add the remaining ingredients, and simmer, uncovered, until the chicken breasts are cooked through, about 5 minutes. Serve on a warm platter with braised escarole.

CHICKEN WITH DATES

FROM PETER HOFFMAN *OF* SAVOY

When chef Peter Hoffman opened Savoy in Soho more than a decade ago, it instantly became a destination for its Mediterranean-inspired cuisine and intimate, cozy atmosphere. Those are precisely the two qualities that make Savoy's Passover seders such a popular annual event. When we were assembling a gourmet Passover menu of updated traditional dishes, Hoffman shared this fragrant, Moroccan-flavored recipe for chicken simmered with dates, honey, and lemon. As it can easily be made in advance and reheated, it's a dish that doesn't require precise timing—an important consideration when a ceremony might take longer than anticipated. But then again, it's delicious enough to become a year-round tradition. SERVES 8

. INGREDIENTS .

2 large chickens, cut into quarters

Salt and freshly ground black pepper

⅓ cup olive oil

3 large onions, peeled and chopped

1 tablespoon ground cinnamon

½ teaspoon ground nutmeg

2 tablespoons honey

3 cups low-fat chicken stock

1 pound dates, pitted and halved lengthwise

Juice of 2 lemons

1 teaspoon saffron

1. Season the chicken parts with salt and a generous amount of pepper. Heat the oil in a large skillet, add the chicken in batches, and brown on all sides over high heat. Remove the chicken and set aside.

2. Add the onion to the skillet and cook over medium heat until soft, about 10 minutes. Add the cinnamon, nutmeg, honey, and stock, and bring to a boil. Reduce the heat and return the chicken to the skillet. Cover and simmer for 25 minutes, or until the chicken is cooked. Skim the fat from the surface. Add the dates, lemon juice, and saffron, and cook for 5 to 10 minutes. Serve the chicken with some of the dates and sauce.

CHICKEN-AND-SHRIMP PAELLA

FROM BOBBY FLAY OF BOLO

After hitting a Southwestern home run at Mesa Grill, Bobby Flay went off on a neo-Spanish tangent at Bolo, his second Manhattan restaurant—but he didn't leave his beloved chili peppers behind. They infuse his splendidly smoky paella recipe, which we've adapted by substituting chicken legs for rabbit. Packed with shrimp, littleneck clams, and chorizo—not to mention ancho and chipotle peppers, saffron, and a megadose of garlic—his version teems with the big, bold flavors that define the famous Flay style. Cook and serve the paella in the same pan for a dramatic party presentation any time of year. NOTE: The paella can be halved and cooked in a 12 inch paella pan. SERVES 8

. INGREDIENTS .

4 whole chicken legs, halved (8 rabbit legs can be substituted)

1 1/2 tablespoons fresh thyme leaves

1/2 cup ancho-chili powder

Salt and black pepper

1/2 cup plus 2 tablespoons extra-virgin olive oil

9 cups chicken stock

3 plum tomatoes, cut into quarters

3 tablespoons honey

1/3 cup minced garlic

1 medium Spanish onion, finely diced

2 chorizo sausages, cut into 1/2-inch slices

4 cups white converted rice

1 tablespoon saffron

1 1/2 tablespoons puréed canned chipotle in adobo

16 littleneck clams, scrubbed

1 1/2 cups fresh baby peas

16 large shrimp, heads on if possible and deveined

1/2 cup chopped fresh parsley, for garnish

1. Rub the chicken with thyme and ancho powder; season with salt and pepper. Place in a bowl and cover. Marinate in the refrigerator for 1 to 2 hours.

2. Heat the 2 tablespoons of oil in a nonstick skillet over medium heat and brown the chicken on both sides, taking care not to burn the ancho powder. Add 2 cups of stock and bring to a simmer. Cover the pan and cook for about 30 minutes, until the meat is very tender. (Transfer to a saucepan if skillet is not large enough to hold all the chicken and the stock.) Drain.

3. While the chicken is cooking, preheat the oven to 450° F.

4. Combine the tomatoes with honey and season with salt and pepper. Place in a small metal bowl and bake for 5 minutes, checking to see that the honey does not burn.

5. In a large paella pan or any wide-mouthed ovenproof pan, heat the 1/2 cup of olive oil over medium to high heat. Add the garlic, onion, and chorizo, and stir until the onion is translucent. Stir in the rice until it is evenly coated with the onion mixture. Add the saffron, chipotle, and 6 cups of stock. Stir well. Reduce the heat to a simmer and cook for 20 minutes.

6. Add the clams, peas, and tomatoes. Cover the pan and cook for 5 minutes. Add the shrimp, chicken, and more stock if necessary (a little liquid should remain). Season to taste and cover again. Cook for 5 more minutes, until the clams are open and the shrimp are cooked. Garnish with chopped parsley.

COQ AU VIN

FROM PHILIPPE ROUSSEL *of* MONTPARNASSE

This coq au vin is as classic as the kitchen from whence it came: Montparnasse, a by-the-book French bistro in midtown Manhattan. It's also a cinch to make, especially when you cook the chicken a day ahead. Truth be told, it tastes even better after it has been reheated, when all the luscious flavors have had enough time to mingle. Instead of using the whole bird, chef Philippe Roussel limits himself to the more flavorful legs and thighs, which he marinates for up to 48 hours in Zinfandel, then briefly cooks in a potent combination of wine and veal demi-glace and garnishes with freshly sautéed mushrooms, bacon, and pearl onions. It's a true classic and a deeply satisfying, surefire crowd pleaser. NOTE: Demi-glace is now available in many gourmet stores. SERVES 6

. INGREDIENTS .

18 chicken legs and thighs
   (9 of each)
2 carrots, cut into 1/2-inch dice
1 rib of celery, cut into 1/2-inch dice
1 large onion, cut into 1/2-inch dice
1 leek, white part only, thinly sliced
2 large sprigs fresh rosemary
4 large sprigs fresh thyme
2 bay leaves
1 tablespoon whole black
   peppercorns, tied in
   cheesecloth

8 cups red wine
   (preferably Zinfandel)
2 tablespoons vegetable oil
5 cups veal demi-glace
   (organic chicken stock
   can be substituted)
1 tablespoon butter, softened
Salt and freshly ground
   black pepper

GARNISHES
3 tablespoons vegetable oil

24 to 30 pearl onions, peeled
   (about 8 ounces)
1/2 cup chicken stock
Salt and freshly ground black pepper
6 ounces slab bacon,
   cut into 1/2-inch cubes
4 ounces shiitake mushrooms caps,
   cut into 1/2-inch-wide slices
4 ounces button mushrooms,
   quartered
6 sprigs fresh thyme or rosemary

1. Put the chicken, carrot, celery, onion, leek, rosemary, thyme, bay leaves, and peppercorns in a large pot and cover completely with 5 cups of wine. Marinate in the refrigerator for 48 hours, turning the chicken occasionally.

2. Strain the vegetables and chicken from the wine, and separate them into two bowls. Reserve the marinade. Pat the chicken dry and season with salt and pepper. Allow the vegetables to drain and dry off.

3. Heat 1 tablespoon of vegetable oil in a large sauté pan over high heat until lightly smoking. Add the chicken, skin side down, in batches to avoid overcrowding, and brown on all sides. Transfer the chicken to a large saucepan or casserole. Heat the remaining tablespoon of oil in the sauté pan, add the vegetables, and sauté over medium heat until they start to brown, about 15 minutes. Add the vegetables to the chicken pieces.

4. Meanwhile, put the reserved marinade in a saucepan and reduce by half. Add the remaining 3 cups of wine and the demi-glace to the saucepan and bring to a low simmer. Pour over the chicken, set the casserole over medium heat, and simmer for 30 minutes. Strain the chicken and vegetables from the liquid, discarding the vegetables, and keep the chicken warm. Return the sauce to the casserole and cook over medium heat until it is reduced by about two-thirds and has thickened (it should coat the back of a wooden spoon). Whisk in the softened butter and season to taste with salt and pepper. When ready to serve, return the chicken to the sauce and bring to a low simmer.

5. GARNISHES: Preheat the oven to 350° F.

6. In a medium ovenproof sauté pan, heat 1 tablespoon of oil until lightly smoking, add the onions, and sauté until

lightly brown. Add the chicken stock, cover the pan with foil, and cook in the oven for 20 minutes, or until the onions are tender when tested with the point of a knife. Season with salt and pepper and set aside

7. Heat 1 tablespoon of oil in another sauté pan, and cook the bacon until it's just golden-brown; do not let it become crisp. Transfer to a bowl and keep warm. Heat

the remaining tablespoon of oil in the same pan until lightly smoking, then add the mushrooms and sauté until soft. Season with salt and pepper and set aside.

8. Transfer the coq au vin to a large serving platter and garnish with the pearl onions, bacon, mushrooms, and sprigs of thyme or rosemary. Serve with mashed potatoes.

THE PERFECT BRINED HERB-ROASTED TURKEY

FROM WALDY MALOUF *OF* BEACON

Waldy Malouf, chef-owner of Beacon in midtown Manhattan, is a bona fide expert on roasting and grilling just about everything. Don't take our word for it. Next Thanksgiving, try this recipe, which we originally published under the supremely confident heading "How to Cook the Perfect Turkey." Eating is believing: Never before had we received such great feedback from home cooks who'd struggled year after year with the big bird, finally finding success (and a scarcity of leftovers) with Malouf's method. First, herb-brining transforms the traditionally dried-out turkey into a succulent treat. Piping a fragrant herb butter between the skin and the breast meat, allowing the turkey to self-baste, doesn't hurt either. And lastly, the bird is stuffed with breakfast sausage, pine nuts, tart apples, and fresh herbs for an additional layer of flavor. It's a technique that carries over into everyday cooking: Ever since testing that recipe, I routinely brine my chickens overnight, transforming ordinary supermarket roasters into something special.

. INGREDIENTS .

BRINE
1 cup sugar
1 cup kosher salt
1 bunch fresh sage
1 bunch fresh thyme
3 tablespoons cracked
    black pepper
One 12-pound turkey (preferably
    organic and free-range)

TURKEY STOCK
Turkey giblets, neck, and
    other trimmings
1 onion, sliced
1 stalk celery, sliced
1 carrot, sliced
2 cloves garlic, sliced
Coarse salt and freshly
    ground pepper
4 cups chicken stock

HERB BUTTER
(make on the day of roasting)
4 ounces (one stick)
    unsalted butter, softened

¼ cup extra-virgin olive oil
1 tablespoon fresh lemon juice
1 tablespoon chopped shallot
1 teaspoon chopped garlic
¼ cup chopped fresh parsley
1 tablespoon chopped fresh chives
1 tablespoon chopped fresh sage
1 tablespoon chopped fresh thyme
1 teaspoon chopped fresh tarragon

SAUSAGE-AND-APPLE STUFFING
1 pound good-quality breakfast
    sausage meat
1 cup chopped onion
2 cloves garlic, minced
2 shallots, chopped
½ cup pine nuts, toasted
2 large tart apples, peeled,
    cored, and cut into ¼-inch dice
1 cup chopped celery
4 tablespoons (½ stick)
    unsalted butter
1 tablespoon chopped fresh thyme

5 large fresh sage leaves, chopped
½ cup dry white wine
1 cup apple cider
One 15-ounce package
    unsweetened bread for stuffing
    or 1 pound stale bread
    cut into ¼-inch cubes
1 extra-large egg
2 cups chicken stock
Coarse salt and freshly ground
    black pepper
2 tablespoons chopped
    fresh parsley

COOKING THE TURKEY
Coarse salt and freshly
    ground pepper
1 onion, sliced
4 stalks celery, sliced
2 carrots, sliced
3 tablespoons unsalted butter
3 tablespoons
    all-purpose flour
1 cup dry white wine

DUCK SCHNITZEL WITH ORANGE-HAZELNUT BROWN BUTTER

FROM PATRICIA YEO *OF* AZ

Patricia Yeo is the only chef we know who holds a master's in biochemistry from Princeton, but her kitchen credentials are equally impressive: Before she opened AZ in 2000, she worked at Bobby Flay's Mesa Grill and Bolo in New York as well as the late Barbara Tropp's China Moon Café in San Francisco. All that diverse experience led to the creation of a unique style that chef Yeo calls California-Asian. Still, that term doesn't do justice to imaginative dishes like this one, which combines French, German, and Asian influences with scrumptious results. Duck breast is an inspired substitute for veal; orange is a classic accompaniment to duck; and a feathery light panko, or Japanese bread-crumb, coating, gives the cutlet an Asian flair. Amazingly, Yeo makes these disparate ideas work and even seem natural. Serve with a tangy watercress-and-arugula salad, tossed with orange segments, which echo the sauce and contrast with the richness of the duck. NOTE: Panko is available in Japanese markets and has recently achieved wider distribution in many Asian markets. Chicken or turkey breast may be substituted for the duck. SERVES 6

. INGREDIENTS .

DUCK SCHNITZEL
6 duck-breast halves, skin removed
3 eggs, beaten
1/2 cup grated Parmesan cheese
2 tablespoons chopped fresh parsley
Salt and freshly ground black pepper
2 to 3 cups panko (available in Asian markets; fresh bread crumbs can be substituted)

6 tablespoons unsalted butter
3/4 cup canola oil

ORANGE-HAZELNUT BROWN BUTTER
4 ounces (1 stick) unsalted butter
1/2 cup chopped hazelnuts, skin removed
1/2 cup fresh orange juice
Zest of 1 orange
Salt and freshly ground black pepper

1. DUCK SCHNITZEL: Split and butterfly each duck-breast half. Place each one between two sheets of plastic wrap. Starting at the center, gently pound out the breast until it is about 1/4-inch thick. Keep refrigerated until ready to use.

2. In a bowl, mix together the eggs, Parmesan, parsley, salt, and pepper. Place the panko in a food processor and pulse two or three times. Put the crushed crumbs in a large, deep bowl. Just before serving, remove the duck from the plastic wrap. Season with pepper. Dip the breast into the egg mixture. Transfer to the bowl with the panko, gently pressing so that the crumbs adhere to

the breast. Remove and shake gently to release any loose crumbs. Repeat with the remaining breasts. (The breaded breasts can be placed on a cookie sheet for up to 10 minutes—after that the breading becomes soggy and will not crisp up as well.)

3. In a large sauté pan over high heat, add 1 tablespoon of butter and 2 tablespoons of canola oil and heat until the butter starts to sizzle and brown slightly. Cook each breast individually until golden-brown (about 2 to 3 minutes on each side). Remove the cooked breast and place on a cookie sheet lined with paper towels. Keep warm while the remaining breasts are cooked.

4. ORANGE-HAZELNUT BROWN BUTTER: Place a sauté pan over high heat, add the butter, and heat until it bubbles and the milk solids start to turn golden-brown. Add the hazelnuts; cook until they are slightly toasted, about 30 seconds. Remove from the heat, add the orange juice and zest, and swirl the pan around until the mixture emulsifies. Season to taste with salt and pepper.

5. Place a schnitzel on each heated plate, pour the orange-hazelnut brown butter sauce over the schnitzel, and serve immediately.

DUCK SHEPHERD'S PIE

FROM LEE HANSON *AND* RIAD NASR *OF* BALTHAZAR

In the fall of 1997, we spotlighted signature dishes from hot new restaurants like Balthazar, the trendsetting Soho brasserie. It was nearly impossible to get a table, but co-chefs Lee Hanson and Riad Nasr gave us the next best thing: their signature recipe for duck shepherd's pie—one of the dishes, like baked beans on toast, that was intended as a tribute of sorts to English-expat owner Keith McNally. After being marinated in red wine for 24 hours, then braised a few more, the intensely flavorful duck meat is pulled off the bone, spooned into individual gratin dishes, topped with root vegetables mashed with butter and cream, and sprinkled with Gruyère. These rich, meaty pies do take some time to assemble, but all the work can be done in advance. And it's still quicker than getting a reservation. SERVES 6

. INGREDIENTS .

6 Moulard duck legs or
    8 Long Island duck legs
2 bottles Cabernet Sauvignon
½ cup ½-inch-diced carrot
½ cup ½-inch-diced celery
½ cup ¼-inch-diced onion
½ cup ½-inch-diced celery root,
    plus 1 whole root
Bouquet garni (6 fresh parsley stems,
    2 or 3 sprigs fresh thyme, and
    1 bay leaf, tied in a cheesecloth)

1 whole head of garlic, halved
    horizontally, plus 4 cloves,
    minced
Salt and freshly ground
    black pepper
2 tablespoons vegetable oil
2 tablespoons tomato paste
3 tablespoons all-purpose flour
3 cups duck, veal, or chicken stock
2 large turnips

4 Yukon Gold potatoes
3 parsnips
¼ cup heavy cream
2 tablespoons unsalted butter
1 cup quartered white
    button mushrooms
1 cup diced shiitake mushroom caps
1 to 2 tablespoons cornstarch
    (optional)
3 to 4 tablespoons grated
    Gruyère cheese

1. Trim the excess fat from the duck legs (do not remove the skin). Put the duck legs, wine, diced vegetables, bouquet garni, and halved head of garlic in a large bowl; cover, and marinate in the refrigerator for 24 hours. Strain the duck legs and vegetables, reserving the marinade.

2. Preheat the oven to 375º F.

3. Season the duck generously with salt and pepper. Heat 1 tablespoon of oil in a large ovenproof skillet and brown the duck. It will render a lot of fat; pour off the excess, reserving 3 to 4 tablespoons in the skillet. Add the diced vegetables and sauté until light brown. Stir in the tomato paste and the flour and cook for several minutes. Add the reserved marinade and reduce by two-thirds. Add the stock and bring to a boil.

4. Cover and cook over low heat or in the oven for 2 to 3 hours, until tender.

5. Peel the turnips, potatoes, celery root, and parsnips, and cut into large chunks. Put in a saucepan, cover with cold water, and add a generous pinch of salt. Cook until tender. Strain the vegetables and pass them through a food mill or mash by hand. Stir in the cream and butter. Season to taste with salt and pepper. Cover with foil and keep warm alongside the stove.

6. When the duck is cooked, strain, reserving the sauce and vegetables, discarding the garlic and bouquet garni. Pull the duck meat from the bones, and break into pieces. Place the meat (and chopped duck skin, if desired) in a large bowl.

7. Reheat the oven to 375º F.

8. Heat 1 tablespoon of oil in a skillet and sauté the minced garlic and mushrooms until soft. Add the mushrooms to the duck, and fold in the diced vegetables and

just enough sauce to cover. (If the sauce seems a little thin, add cornstarch dissolved in a little water, and heat the sauce until thickened enough to bind with the duck and vegetables.) Spoon into individual gratin cishes and spread the root purée over the duck-and-vegetable mixture. Sprinkle with Gruyère and bake for 30 to 35 minutes. Serve hot with the remaining sauce on the side.

MEAT LOAF WITH MUSHROOM SAUCE

FROM TOM VALENTI *of* OUEST

Comfort food never seems to go out of style. As soon as we published the recipe for Tom Valenti's famous meat loaf, the one that has garnered a devoted Sunday-night following at Ouest, his popular American bistro, it seemed like the whole city had put it to sauce-splattered, dog-eared use. Valenti combines ground beef, veal, and pork and adds crushed saltines for an unusually light texture. But the real secret to his success is bacon, and lots of it: Valenti cloaks the free-form loaf with thinly sliced strips, which baste and flavor the meat as it cooks. At Ouest, he simmers the stock for his mushroom sauce for hours; our time-saving adaptation achieves the same deeply flavored effect by incorporating ground porcini mushrooms. Equally delicious hot or cold, this meat loaf may give leftovers an even better name. SERVES 6 TO 8

. INGREDIENTS .

1 tablespoon olive oil
1 medium Spanish onion, finely chopped
3 cloves garlic, minced
2 eggs, beaten
1/2 teaspoon chopped fresh thyme leaves
3 tablespoons plus 1 teaspoon Dijon mustard
2 tablespoons Worcestershire sauce
1/2 teaspoon Tabasco sauce
1 cup milk
2 pounds ground meat (equal parts beef, pork, and veal preferred)
2/3 cup crushed saltines
1/4 cup minced fresh flat-leaf parsley

1 tablespoon coarse salt
1 teaspoon freshly ground black pepper
6 ounces thinly sliced bacon (optional)
Mushroom Sauce (recipe follows)

MUSHROOM SAUCE
3 tablespoons unsalted butter
2 cloves garlic, minced
2 portobello mushrooms, cut into 3/8-inch cubes
One 16-ounce can low-sodium beef broth
1 ounce dried porcini mushrooms, ground to dust in a coffee grinder
1 tablespoon Wondra flour

1. Preheat the oven to 350º F.

2. Pour the oil into a sauté pan and set over medium-high heat. Add the onion and garlic and sauté until translucent, about 5 minutes. Remove from the heat and allow to cool.

3. In a mixing bowl, stir together the eggs, thyme, mustard, Worcestershire sauce, Tabasco sauce, and milk.

4. Place the ground meat into another bowl and pour the egg mixture over the meat. Add the saltines, parsley, onion, and garlic to the bowl. Season with salt and pepper.

5. Roll up your sleeves, and knead the meat together with the other ingredients until well blended (if you like, cook a small portion of the mixture in a pan, taste, and adjust the seasoning).

6. Transfer to a cookie sheet and form into a loaf. If using the bacon, wrap the slices lengthwise over the top and tuck them under the loaf, to cover the meat completely. Bake for 1 hour or until an instant-read thermometer inserted into the center of the loaf reads 160º F. Remove from the oven and set aside to rest for 5 minutes. Slice and serve with mushroom sauce and mashed potatoes.

7. MUSHROOM SAUCE: Heat 2 tablespoons of the butter in a sauté pan, add the garlic and portobello mushrooms, and sauté until soft. Bring the broth to a boil in a saucepan, and reduce by a quarter. Remove from the heat and add the ground porcini.

8. Mix the flour and 4 tablespoons of water in a bowl, stirring until combined. Add the sautéed mushrooms and flour to the porcini broth, set the saucepan over low heat, and stir until the broth thickens. Stir in the remaining tablespoon of butter just before serving.

OXTAIL RIOJA

FROM DANIEL BOULUD *OF* CAFÉ BOULUD

Café Boulud is a more casual alternative—barely—to four-star Restaurant Daniel, built on executive chef Daniel Boulud's memories of his grandparents' restaurant just outside Lyon. But here, the clever menu is divided into four sections: La Tradition, La Saison, Le Potager, and Le Voyage. The latter allows the chef to explore the cuisines of various parts of the world, including Spain, from whence comes this hearty oxtail Rioja. First, the oxtail is dusted with paprika, then it's braised with smoky Serrano ham, green frying peppers, tomatoes, and Rioja, until the flavors come together to form a rich, gelatinous sauce and the meat is falling-off-the-bone tender. Serve it with mashed potatoes and you will realize why this is one of Boulud's favorite dishes—and mine. NOTE: Like any stew, this can be made a day ahead, allowing the flavors to develop and the fat to separate. Before reheating, any fat that has formed on the surface should be removed. Oxtail is a very bony cut, and you might find it difficult to remove the meat unless the oxtail is cooked well—almost falling off the bone. Depending on the size of the pieces of oxtail, it might need a little longer than the recipe states. Prosciutto di Parma can be substituted for the Serrano ham. SERVES 8

. INGREDIENTS .

6 pounds oxtail, cut into 2-inch-thick pieces
1 ½ tablespoons sweet paprika
Salt and freshly ground black pepper
3 tablespoons all-purpose flour
¼ cup olive oil
¼ pound Serrano ham, sliced ½ inch thick, cut into ½-inch dice
1 head garlic, cut in half crosswise
1 large onion, peeled and cut into ¼-inch dice
1 large carrot, peeled and cut into ¼-inch dice

1 pound green frying peppers, seeded and cut into ½-inch dice
1 tablespoon tomato paste
1 pound fresh tomatoes, halved lengthwise, cored, seeded, and cut into eighths
Bouquet garni (1 bay leaf, 2 sprigs fresh parsley, 2 sprigs fresh thyme tied in cheesecloth)
6 cups Rioja wine
1 ½ quarts chicken stock
½ cup sliced almonds, toasted, for garnish

1. Season the oxtail with the paprika, salt, and pepper, then dredge in flour, shaking off the excess. Heat the oil in a large skillet over medium heat. When hot, add some of the oxtail—do not overcrowd the skillet—and cook, turning, until the pieces are brown on each side, about 10 minutes. Repeat with the remaining oxtail. Transfer the oxtail to a plate and pour off all but 2 tablespoons of the fat in the pan. Add the ham, garlic, onion, carrot, and green pepper to the skillet. Cook, stirring, for 15 minutes, or until the vegetables are tender.

2. Stir in the tomato paste and tomatoes. Return the oxtail to the pan, adding the bouquet garni and the red wine. Bring to a boil, skimming the foam that rises to the surface, and cook until the wine is reduced by half. Add the chicken stock and bring to a boil, then adjust the heat until simmering. Cover and cook for 2 ½ hours, checking the pan every 30 minutes to make sure the liquid is not boiling and skimming any foam that appears on the surface. Remove the cover and continue to simmer for 30 minutes, or until the sauce is reduced and thickened—it should coat the oxtail. Remove from heat. Remove and discard the bouquet garni and the garlic, and sprinkle the oxtail with the almonds.

CHATEAUBRIAND WITH PORTOBELLO-BACON SAUCE

FROM RICK LAAKKONEN *OF* ILO

This recipe comes from Rick Laakkonen, the inventive chef at Ilo in the Bryant Park Hotel, and formerly at Brooklyn's landmark River Café. His seven-course, all-beef tasting menu, "For Beef Lovers Only," was a huge hit among diehard carnivores when he introduced it at Ilo. This chateaubriand for six is equally impressive, perfect for when the occasion calls for a show-stopping dish that's both festive and homey. When attempting to up the flavor ante, the addition of bacon to a recipe never hurts. Laakkonen adds the magic ingredient to a mushroom sauce that does the trick, adding great depth of flavor. Unless you want to serve it at room temperature, the beef should be seared and roasted at the last moment, but the sauce can be made ahead of time and reheated later. And don't worry if you have any leftovers—they're great for sandwiches the next day. SERVES 6

. INGREDIENTS .

PORTOBELLO-BACON SAUCE

8 ¼ cups beef broth (low-sodium if using canned)

1 bottle Merlot (or other red wine with mellow tannins)

½ cup canola oil

4 ounces sliced double-smoked bacon,
    cut in half lengthwise and julienned

5 shallots, finely diced

8 to 10 portobello mushroom caps,
    peeled and cut into ¼-inch dice

1 teaspoon finely chopped fresh thyme

3 tablespoons cornstarch or arrowroot

1 tablespoon unsalted butter

Salt and freshly ground black pepper

CHATEAUBRIAND

4 to 4 ½ pounds beef tenderloin, trimmed
    (with the thin tail end folded to equalize
    the thickness) and tied at 1½-inch intervals

1. PORTOBELLO-BACON SAUCE: Place 8 cups of the broth in a saucepan over medium heat and reduce to about 2 cups. In a separate saucepan, reduce the red wine to about 1 cup.

2. Heat ¼ cup of the oil in a large pan, then add the bacon and cook until it's crisp but not burned; remove and set aside. Add the shallots to the pan, cook until translucent, and stir in the diced mushrooms. When the mushrooms have released all their liquid, return the bacon to the pan, add the reduced wine, and bring to a simmer. Add the reduced beef broth and thyme and simmer for 30 minutes. Mix the cornstarch or arrowroot with the remaining ¼ cup of beef broth and add to the sauce after the first 15 minutes of cooking. When ready to serve,

whisk in the butter and season with salt and pepper. If the sauce becomes too thick, thin it out with a little water.

3. CHATEAUBRIAND: Preheat the oven to 400° F.

4. Season the meat generously with salt and pepper. Heat the remaining ¼ cup of oil in a large ovenproof sauté pan. When the oil begins to smoke, add the tenderloin and sear on all sides. Place the pan in the oven and roast for 20 to 30 minutes, to desired doneness (115 to 118° F for rare, 120° F for medium rare). Remove from the oven, cover loosely with foil, and allow to rest for 20 minutes. Cut into 1-inch-thick slices and serve two per person with the portobello-bacon sauce. Hearts of celery, organic carrots, leeks, and Bintje potatoes—all braised—make great accompaniments.

PORK SHOULDER BRAISED IN STOUT

FROM GRAY KUNZ *OF* LESPINASSE

During his renowned tenure at Lespinasse in the St. Regis Hotel, Gray Kunz was best known for his daring Franco-Asian innovations. In the mid-nineties, he showed a different side of his culinary personality by introducing a bistro menu in the adjacent Astor Court, featuring simpler rustic fare, like this whole pork shoulder braised in stout and maple syrup. The shoulder is an inexpensive cut that requires long, slow cooking—three hours, to be precise—after which the meat and accompanying root vegetables are equally tender and succulent. The bitterness of the stout might seem a bit overwhelming at first, but it slowly mellows into a rich, aromatic sauce that demands some starch to sop it up. Kunz is partial to spaetzle—he's Swiss, after all— but mashed potatoes work just as well. SERVES 8

· INGREDIENTS ·

¾ pound celery root, peeled

5 medium carrots, peeled

1¼ pounds onions, peeled

3 cloves

½ teaspoon allspice berries

1 tablespoon black peppercorns

1 teaspoon juniper berries

1 sprig fresh parsley

1 sprig fresh rosemary

3 sprigs fresh thyme

6 pounds pork shoulder or butt, all skin removed

Salt and freshly ground black pepper

6 tablespoons corn oil

3 cloves garlic, peeled

¾ cup maple syrup

6 tablespoons white wine vinegar

3 cups stout (two 12-ounce bottles)

2 ⅓ cups veal stock or water

2 tablespoons chopped mix of fresh parsley, chives, and tarragon

2 tablespoons unsalted butter

1 tablespoon ½-inch-long fresh chives, for garnish

8 to 10 celery leaves, for garnish

1. Cut the celery root, carrots, and onions into 2-inch pieces. Using a square of cheesecloth and a piece of string, make a small sachet containing the cloves, allspice, peppercorns, and juniper berries. Tie the parsley, rosemary, and thyme sprigs together with a piece of string to create a bouquet garni.

2. Preheat the oven to 300° F.

3. Season the pork with salt and pepper. Heat the oil in a large skillet and sear the pork on all sides; remove and place in a large casserole. Sauté the vegetables and garlic in the skillet until just starting to brown. Put the mixture in the casserole with the pork. Deglaze the skillet with the maple syrup and vinegar; reduce by half. Add the stout and stock; bring to a boil and pour over the pork and vegetables. Add the spice sachet and the bundle of herbs to the casserole, and bring to a boil. Cover and place in the oven for 3 hours. Baste and turn the meat every 30 minutes.

4. When cooked, remove the meat, strain the liquid, and keep the vegetables with the pork, covered, in a warm oven. Reduce the liquid to a third in a saucepan over medium-high heat. Remove from the heat and stir in the chopped herbs and butter. Season to taste. Arrange the meat and vegetables on a large platter. Pour the sauce over the meat and baste until the meat is glazed. Garnish the pork with chives and celery leaves.

Grilled Eggplant and Feta Salad (page 124)

THE PERFECT GRILLED STEAK

FROM DAVID WALZOG OF MICHAEL JORDAN'S THE STEAK HOUSE NYC

Is it possible to achieve the perfect New York steak house steak in your own backyard on a plain old Weber grill? This was the big question we asked in our summer entertaining issue of 1999. "YES!" came the definitive answer from David Walzog, executive chef of Michael Jordan's, one of the city's best steak houses, located inside the beautifully restored Grand Central Terminal. Like many chef's secrets, this one is incredibly simple: Dip the steak in a mixture of corn oil and clarified butter, then rub both sides generously with cracked black pepper and kosher salt. Whatever you do, don't stint on the salt—that's what gives the cut its exquisite steakhouse char and keeps the meat medium rare and juicy within.

Whether he's at work or at home, Walzog starts with the best prime-grade, dry-aged beef. You can substitute a 1½-inch-thick choice steak from the grocery store, but you won't get the same depth of flavor. Walzog looks for meat with the most marbling, i.e., visible grains of fat running through the steak. As the steak is cooking, the fat melts, naturally tenderizing the meat and building in flavor. (He avoids vein steaks—the ones with a half-moon-shaped vein running through the cut—because they're too tough.)

At home, Walzog uses a Weber charcoal grill, stacking approximately thirty-five pieces of charcoal in the center. He lets the fire burn for 15 to 20 minutes, until the coals turn about halfway white; then he spreads them out to one side, leaving a cool spot on the other. Next, he covers the grill with the lid, top vent open, for 3 to 5 minutes, until it's seriously hot—hot enough to sear the outside quickly and form a crust. The goal—the perfect steak—is defined by the contrast between the charred exterior and the warm, juicy center. SERVES 4

• INGREDIENTS •

8 ounces (2 sticks) unsalted butter
4 prime New York strip steaks (1 ½ inches thick,
    about 14 to 16 ounces each; the thickness
    is more important than the weight)
½ cup corn oil
8 teaspoons kosher salt
8 teaspoons cracked black pepper
Chili Rub (optional; recipe follows)
Herb Rub (optional; recipe follows)

CHILI RUB
1 tablespoon ancho-chili powder
1 teaspoon ground cumin

1 teaspoon ground coriander
1 teaspoon garlic powder
1 teaspoon cayenne
1 tablespoon kosher salt

HERB RUB
1 tablespoon dried thyme
1 tablespoon dried oregano
1 tablespoon ground fennel seeds
1 tablespoon kosher salt
2 teaspoons mustard powder
1 teaspoon onion powder
2 teaspoons Spanish paprika

1. Melt the butter over medium-high heat, and skim the milk solids from the surface using a spoon. Set aside to cool.

2. Remove the steaks from the refrigerator about 30 to 40 minutes before cooking. Cover them loosely with plastic wrap and allow the steaks to come to room

BARBECUED RIBS

FROM PATRICK CLARK *OF* TAVERN ON THE GREEN

New York-bred, French-trained Patrick Clark was one of America's most renowned African-American chefs in the eighties and nineties. Two Manhattan landmarks bookended his career—the trendsetting Odeon and the gargantuan Tavern on the Green, where the succulent barbecued ribs he served in the garden became more of a summertime attraction than the famous topiary. After a trip to Kansas City, where he ate his way through that 'cue capital's hot spots, he concocted his own spice rub, which he combined with vinegar to make a paste to massage into the ribs. After marinating overnight, they're first slow-baked in a low oven to make them fall-off-the-bone tender, and then slicked with Clark's tangy barbecue sauce and quickly grilled for an irresistibly smoky flavor. Get out the Wet-Naps, roll up your sleeves, and dig in. SERVES 6

. INGREDIENTS .

3 to 4 tablespoons Rib-Rub Spice (recipe follows)
¼ cup white wine vinegar
2 slabs pork ribs (each 3 pounds or smaller), flaps removed
Barbecue Sauce (recipe follows)

RIB-RUB SPICE
4 tablespoons sweet paprika
2 tablespoons Old Bay seasoning
1 teaspoon cayenne
2 tablespoons chili powder

2 teaspoons salt
2 teaspoons garlic powder
1 tablespoon sugar

BARBECUE SAUCE
1 onion, chopped
2 cups fresh orange juice
4 cups ketchup
½ cup fresh lime juice
½ cup cider vinegar
¼ cup light brown sugar
1 tablespoon salt
1 tablespoon black pepper

2 tablespoons dry mustard
2 tablespoons sweet paprika
¾ to 1 tablespoon crushed red-pepper flakes, to taste
1 teaspoon garlic powder
1 teaspoon chili powder
1 to 2 tablespoons Tabasco, to taste
2 tablespoons tamarind paste
2 tablespoons honey
6 ounces (1 ½ sticks) unsalted butter

1. Combine the rib-rub spice with the vinegar in a bowl to make a paste. Rub into the ribs and wrap in plastic. Refrigerate overnight.

2. Preheat the oven to 250º F.

3. Remove the plastic from the ribs and place them on a foil-lined baking sheet. Bake in the oven for 3 hours. Do not turn during cooking.

4. Remove the ribs from the oven and allow to rest. Heat the grill until the coals are red-hot. Coat the top side of the ribs with barbecue sauce, grill for 5 minutes, turn and brush with sauce, and cook for 5 more minutes, taking care not to burn, as the sugar in the barbecue sauce caramelizes quickly.

5. RIB-RUB SPICE: Sift all of the ingredients into a bowl and combine well. Store in an airtight jar. Use on ribs or chicken.

6. BARBECUE SAUCE: Place the onion and ½ cup of the orange juice in a blender and purée until smooth. Transfer to a medium-size saucepan. Add the remaining ingredients to the saucepan and bring to a boil. Simmer for 25 to 30 minutes. Set aside to cool. The sauce will keep for two weeks, covered, in the refrigerator.

SPICY GRILL-STEAMED CLAMS

FROM PETER KLEIN *OF* CHOW BAR

Before he opened Chow Bar in Manhattan's West Village, Peter Klein cooked at the ultra-hot China Grill, where he became a master of pan-Asian flavors and the sort of exotic seasonings that give these clams a real kick. He wraps them in foil packets with sake, butter, ginger, and garlic, then buries the sealed packets in the burning coals of a hot grill. After ten minutes or so, the clams steam open, releasing their briny juices into the red pepper-flecked broth. When the packets are unwrapped, they give entirely new meaning to the word aromatherapy. SERVES 6

. INGREDIENTS .

¾ cup dry sake or beer

1½ teaspoons minced fresh ginger

1½ teaspoons minced garlic

1 teaspoon crushed red pepper

3 scallions, sliced on the bias

3 pounds Manila clams, washed thoroughly (about 54 clams)

3 tablespoons unsalted butter

3 tablespoons chopped fresh cilantro, for garnish

1½ limes, quartered, for garnish

Chili Toast (recipe follows)

CHILI TOAST

½ cup olive oil

2 tablespoons hot paprika

1 loaf of crusty bread, cut into ½-inch-thick slices

1. Light a charcoal grill.

2. Cut three pieces of heavy-duty foil, approximately 12 x 24 inches each, and fold each in half to form a square. Fold up the sides of each to form a makeshift pot. Divide the ingredients into thirds. In the bottom of each foil "pot," stir together a third of the sake, ginger, garlic, red pepper, and scallions. Top with clams and butter and seal the tops of the foil. Place the foil packets directly on the hot coals and steam for 10 to 12 minutes. Remove from the heat, open the packets, and sprinkle with cilantro. Serve with lime wedges and grilled chili toast. Each packet serves two.

3. CHILI TOAST: Whisk together the oil and paprika and brush both sides of the bread with the oil. Place on the rack of the barbecue, grill on both sides until toasted (about 1 or 2 minutes), and serve with the clams.

7
VEGETABLES
AND SIDES

Heirloom Tomato-and-Watermelon Salad (page 139)

ROASTED ROOT VEGETABLES

FROM WALDY MALOUF *OF* BEACON

During the winter there is nothing quite like the comfort and ease of oven-roasting meats and vegetables as the mouthwatering aromas waft through the kitchen. Beacon chef Waldy Malouf has perfected a method of roasting winter root vegetables, allowing them to caramelize and using balsamic vinegar to intensify their flavor. For Thanksgiving, he suggests cooking them before the turkey and serving them at room temperature, but they're a wonderful accompaniment to any roast meat. Feel free to experiment with the ingredients depending on what you find in the market, but remember that beets, sweet potatoes, and carrots make a colorful contrast to the paler vegetables. SERVES 8

. INGREDIENTS .

2 parsnips	2 sweet potatoes
4 carrots	1 cup salsify (optional)
1 large celery root	3 tablespoons olive oil
1 medium rutabaga	1½ cups chicken stock
2 turnips	⅓ cup balsamic vinegar
2 beets	Salt and freshly ground black pepper

1. Preheat oven to 350° F.

2. Peel the vegetables and cut them into 1½-inch wedges or lengths.

3. Bring a saucepan of salted water to a boil. Add the salsify and cook for 1 minute. Drain and plunge into a bowl of iced water. Drain again.

4. Select a roasting pan or casserole that will hold the vegetables in one layer. Film the pan with the oil, add the vegetables, and toss them in the oil. Roast the vegetables, turning once or twice, for about ½ hour.

5. Pour the stock and vinegar over the vegetables. Cover the pan with foil and continue to roast for 45 to 60 minutes, or until the vegetables are soft, turning them occasionally to make sure the vegetables do not stick to the pan. Uncover the pan and continue to cook the vegetables until most of the liquid has evaporated. Season with salt and pepper. Serve at room temperature.

8
DESSERTS

Crème Fraîche Panna Cotta with Strawberry Purée (page 166)

APPLE PIE WITH A CHEDDAR CRUST

FROM WALDY MALOUF *OF* BEACON

In the fall, right before Thanksgiving, when the Union Square Greenmarket is bursting at the seams with a huge variety of apples at their peak of flavor, a young chef's thoughts turn to—what else?—apple pie and Mom. Or at least, that's the case with Beacon's Waldy Malouf. His mother's version of the quintessential all-American classic includes a Cheddar crust, and Dad, Waldy Sr., always sprinkles more cheese over his own slice. Keeping the family tradition alive, Malouf now makes a version of Mom's pie at home with his own daughter. The sharp cheese gives the crust a superior crunch and adds just the right counterpoint to the sweet-tart flavor of the apples. If you want more Cheddar, do what Waldy Sr. does, or serve an extra slice of cheese on the side. SERVES 6 TO 8

. INGREDIENTS .

PIE CRUST

1 3/4 cups all-purpose flour, sifted

1/4 teaspoon coarse salt

1 cup grated good-quality sharp cheddar cheese
(about 1/4 pound)

6 ounces (1 1/2 sticks) cold unsalted butter,
cut into 8 pieces

1 large egg

FILLING

5 or 6 large tart apples, such as McIntosh or
Cortland, peeled, cored, and sliced thin

1/2 bourbon vanilla bean, split lengthwise
(regular vanilla bean can be substituted)

Juice of 1/2 lemon

1/2 teaspoon coarse salt

3/4 cup light brown sugar

2 tablespoons all-purpose flour

1. CRUST: Put the flour, salt, and cheese into the bowl of a food processor and pulse three to four times, until the cheese is finely chopped and evenly distributed. Add the butter and pulse three to four times, until the mixture has the consistency of cornmeal. (It should not be smooth.) Transfer the mixture to a medium-size bowl. Make a well in the center of the flour mixture and break in the egg. Using a fork, stir the egg into the flour mixture. With your hands, knead the dough into a mass, then divide it into two balls, one slightly larger than the other. Pat and spread the larger ball of dough into a 9-inch pie plate. Place the remaining dough between two pieces of waxed paper, and roll to form the top crust. Refrigerate or freeze both crusts, covered, for at least 2 hours.

2. Preheat the oven to 375° F.

3. Remove the pastry from the refrigerator or freezer 1/2 hour before baking.

4. FILLING: Put the apples and vanilla bean in a bowl, squeeze the lemon over them, and sprinkle on the salt, sugar, and flour. Using your hands, mix the filling thoroughly and pile it into the pie crust. Cover the apples with the top crust. Dip your finger in water and run it along the pie plate between the two crusts, then crimp the edges and trim the crust. Slash the top crust or cut a decorative shape out of the pastry to allow the steam to escape, and bake the pie on the bottom shelf of the oven for 1/2 hour. Lay a piece of foil loosely over the pie, and bake for another 20 to 25 minutes, or until the juices are bubbling and the fruit is tender (stick a knife through the opening in the crust to see if it is done). Serve warm, with or without extra cheese.

CHILLED WATERMELON SOUP WITH YUZU

FROM ROCCO DISPIRITO *OF* UNION PACIFIC

Before he opened Union Pacific, Rocco DiSpirito worked with Gray Kunz at Lespinasse, and under his mentor's intoxicating French-Asian influence, DiSpirito began to develop a signature fusion style of his own. He has been astounding New Yorkers with his farfetched flavor combinations ever since. Even desserts undergo an Asian-inspired alchemy, as in this chilled watermelon soup enlivened with lemon zest, lemongrass, tangerine sorbet, and the Japanese citrus juice—yuzu—a most refreshing change of pace from summer's run-of-the-mill cold soups. SERVES 6

. INGREDIENTS .

½ cup plus 3 tablespoons sugar

2 teaspoons each lemon, lime, and orange zest, blanched

2 stalks lemongrass, cut into thirds and crushed

3 pounds watermelon plus ½ cup small watermelon balls

2 tablespoons yuzu juice

Tangerine or clementine sorbet

1. Heat ½ cup of the sugar and 1 cup of water in a small saucepan for 5 minutes; add the citrus zest and simmer until tender. Remove from the heat; allow the zest to marinate in the syrup for 12 hours. Strain through a sieve and reserve the candied zest.

2. Add the remaining 3 tablespoons of sugar to 1 cup of water in a small saucepan, and boil until the sugar dissolves. Add the lemongrass and simmer for 15 minutes. Remove from the heat and allow to infuse for 2 hours.

3. Cut the watermelon into pieces, and purée in a blender or food processor in batches. Pass the purée through a fine sieve.

4. Combine the watermelon liquid and yuzu juice, and sweeten to taste with the strained lemongrass syrup. Serve with melon and sorbet balls and garnish with candied zest.

GINGERBREAD-MASCARPONE TRIFLE WITH CANDIED KUMQUATS, CRANBERRIES, AND PISTACHIOS

FROM CLAUDIA FLEMING *OF* GRAMERCY TAVERN

When Claudia Fleming was the pastry chef at Gramercy Tavern, gingerbread in various inventive guises was a recurring motif on her winter menu. (A Guinness-and-coffee-spiked version enjoyed a particularly rabid following.) For our holiday issue one year, she dressed it up for the occasion in this show-stopping trifle, a festive twist on the traditional English dessert. As always, she incorporates seasonal ingredients like cranberries and kumquats, which lend a sweet, tart contrast to the spicy cake. Geared specifically for the home cook, this recipe is easier than it looks—each step can be completed in advance, and the taste actually improves as the gingerbread softens and the flavors develop. SERVES 10 TO 12

. INGREDIENTS .

GINGERBREAD
1 cup Guinness stout
1 cup molasses
1/2 cup brewed coffee
1 teaspoon baking soda
1 tablespoon grated fresh ginger
2 1/2 cups all-purpose flour
1 tablespoon baking powder
1 tablespoon cocoa powder
2 teaspoons ground ginger
1 1/4 teaspoons ground cinnamon

Generous pinch each of ground
  nutmeg, cloves, and white pepper
8 tablespoons (1 stick) butter
1 1/4 cups packed dark-brown sugar
1 egg

MASCARPONE CREAM
14 ounces mascarpone
14 ounces whipping cream
6 ounces goat's-milk yogurt (regular
  plain yogurt can be substituted)

1/2 cup plus 1 tablespoon sugar
1 1/2 tablespoons Grand Marnier

CANDIED FRUIT
5 1/2 cups sugar
2 pounds kumquats, 1 1/2 pounds
  cut into 4 slices each,
  1/2 pound left whole
1 1/2 cups whole green
  shelled pistachios (unsalted)
1 cup fresh cranberries

1. GINGERBREAD: Preheat the oven to 350° F.

2. Butter and flour two 8-inch cake pans (1 1/2 inches deep).

3. In a large, heavy-bottomed saucepan, bring the beer, molasses, and coffee to a boil (carefully, as the mixture has a tendency to foam up suddenly). Remove from the heat and add the baking soda; the mixture will foam up again. Set aside to cool to room temperature. When cool, add the grated ginger.

4. In a large bowl, sift together the flour, baking powder, cocoa, ground ginger, cinnamon, nutmeg, cloves, and white pepper.

5. In another large bowl, cream the butter and sugar together until light and fluffy. Beat in the egg. Add the dry and wet ingredients to the creamed mixture alternately, beginning and ending with the dry ingredients.

6. Divide the batter between the cake pans and bake for about 1 hour, until the cake springs back when touched

CHOCOLATE BROWNIES

FROM CLAUDIA FLEMING *OF* GRAMERCY TAVERN

Everyone has a favorite brownie recipe, but Claudia Fleming's brownies are tough to beat. We featured them in our comfort food issue published shortly after September 11, 2001, when home cooking and baking became a makeshift form of therapy. Claudia considers chocolate one of the most comforting things to eat (who doesn't?), and when she wasn't crafting elegant desserts at Gramercy Tavern, all she wanted was to be ensconced in her own kitchen, baking these intensely rich and outrageously nutty brownies. She recommends using dark chocolate from Scharffen Berger, the artisanal American manufacturer. It's intensely chocolatey but not overly sweet, and in Claudia's expert opinion, the better the chocolate, the better the brownie. NOTE: Expect a subtly different flavor if you substitute Callebaut, Valrhona, or any other high-quality chocolate. SERVES 6 TO 8

. INGREDIENTS .

8 ounces (2 sticks) unsalted butter,
    plus additional for greasing the pan
4 ounces high-quality unsweetened
    chocolate (preferably Scharffen Berger)
2 large eggs
1 ²/₃ cups sugar

1 teaspoon vanilla extract
1 cup all-purpose flour
½ teaspoon salt
²/₃ cup coarsely chopped pecans
    (or ⅓ cup pecans and
    ⅓ cup semisweet chocolate chips)

1. Preheat the oven to 350° F.

2. Melt the butter and chocolate in a bowl set over a saucepan of simmering water.

3. In a large bowl, beat the eggs, sugar, and vanilla until combined. Add the melted butter and chocolate, and whisk until incorporated. Fold in the flour and salt, and finally stir in the nuts.

4. Pour into a greased 9 x 9-inch pan and bake for approximately 35 minutes, or until it's just pulling away from the sides; the center should be very moist but not runny.

5. Allow to cool in the pan before cutting. Best served when the brownies have rested for several hours.

STEAMED LEMON PUDDING WITH BERRY COMPOTE

FROM KAREN DEMASCO *OF* CRAFT

After understudying pastry whiz Claudia Fleming at Gramercy Tavern, Karen DeMasco followed Gramercy Tavern chef Tom Colicchio around the corner to his new restaurant, Craft, where she took her confectionery cues from his hyperseasonal, ingredient-driven menu. When she first mentioned the words "steamed lemon pudding," I recoiled from the memory of those heavy, suet-laden steamed puddings I grew up with in England. But Karen's buttermilk-enriched version is light and tangy, with a pleasingly mouth-puckering lemony flavor and not a scrap of suet. Happily, that was lost in the translation. SERVES 8

. INGREDIENTS .

PUDDING
Softened unsalted butter for ramekins
¾ cup granulated sugar plus additional for ramekins
1 cup buttermilk
¼ cup fresh lemon juice
3 eggs, separated
¼ cup plus 1 tablespoon all-purpose flour

¼ teaspoon salt
Zest of 2 lemons, finely chopped

BERRY COMPOTE
2 cups blueberries
2 cups raspberries
¼ cup sugar

1. Preheat the oven to 325º F.

2. PUDDING: Grease the insides of eight 4-ounce ramekins with butter and coat with sugar.

3. In a mixing bowl, combine the buttermilk, lemon juice, and the egg yolks. In another bowl, mix the flour, remaining ¾ cup of sugar, salt, and lemon zest. Whip the egg whites in a third bowl until soft peaks form. Whisk the dry ingredients with the buttermilk mixture, and fold in the egg whites gently, a third at a time. Ladle the batter into the prepared ramekins, filling them almost to the top. Place the ramekins in a roasting pan, and pour warm water around them until it comes halfway up the sides of the ramekins. Cover with foil and bake for 18 minutes, or until the pudding begins to rise slightly. Remove the foil, rotate the pan front to back, and bake for another 20 to 25 minutes, until the pudding is golden and springs back when touched.

4. COMPOTE : While the pudding is baking, place the blueberries in a saucepan with the sugar and cook over medium heat until the berries just start to burst. Remove from the heat and fold in the raspberries.

5. Serve the puddings at room temperature or reheat in a warm-water bath before inverting onto plates and surrounding with compote.

INDIVIDUAL RASPBERRY SOUFFLÉS

FROM JACQUES TORRES *OF* LE CIRQUE 2000

Few desserts are as impressive as a classic soufflé, so you might be tempted to trot these raspberry babies out on very special occasions. But you'll be happy to know—even if your guests never do—just how foolproof they actually are. The recipe comes from Jacques Torres, who spent years perfecting it as pastry chef at Le Cirque 2000 before he left to open a chocolate factory in Brooklyn. During his heady soufflé days, he devised a method to make them ahead of time, letting them sit for several hours before cooking them to order. His trick was to mix Italian meringue with barely cooked raspberries that had been stabilized with pectin, but here, he substitutes regular meringue to simplify matters for the home cook. NOTE: Do not overwork the egg whites when adding the raspberry. Never open the oven while the soufflés are cooking, and when they're done, serve them immediately. If you prefer to make one large 8-inch (1½-quart) soufflé, it should be baked in a 375° F oven for about 20 to 25 minutes. SERVES 6

. INGREDIENTS .

1 tablespoon unsalted butter, softened	2 tablespoons Sure-Jell (pectin)
1 cup plus 5 tablespoons granulated sugar	8 large egg whites
9 ounces (2 heaping cups) fresh raspberries	Confectioners' sugar for dusting

1. Preheat the oven to 400° F.

2. Coat the insides of six 1-cup soufflé molds with the softened butter. Sprinkle 1 tablespoon of the granulated sugar into one of the molds and roll it around to coat, pouring the excess into the next mold and repeating.

3. Place the raspberries, ½ cup plus 2 tablespoons of the granulated sugar, and the Sure-Jell in a small saucepan, and whisk over medium-high heat until the mixture boils. Boil for about 1 or 2 minutes, until it thickens and the fruit breaks down. Keep the mixture warm.

4. Meanwhile, place the egg whites in a large mixing bowl and whip with an electric mixer on low speed until foamy. Begin adding the remaining granulated sugar, a little at a time. Increase the speed to high, continuing to add sugar, and whip the whites to stiff and shiny but not dry peaks.

5. Fold the warm raspberry mixture into the meringue in two additions until just combined (you may still see flecks of raspberry), being careful not to overmix or deflate the whites.

6. Using a rubber spatula, gently spoon the soufflé mixture into the molds, mounding them about 1 inch over the rims of the molds. The unbaked soufflés will hold at room temperature for about an hour before baking.

7. Set the molds on a baking sheet and place in the center of the oven with a clear space above. Bake until the soufflés rise and start to brown on top, about 10 to 12 minutes. Remove from the oven and dust the tops with confectioners' sugar. Serve immediately.

ESPRESSO GRANITA

FROM **CHRISTOPHER GARGONE** OF **REMI**

In anticipation of the scorching summer of 1995, we featured Christopher Gargone, the former pastry chef of Remi, and his heavenly granitas—or, as we called them at the time, sno-cones for grownups. Gargone came up with several inspired combinations, such as lemon-mint, grapefruit-Campari, and Burgundy-orange, all intensely flavored and delicious, but this classic espresso granita is our favorite. Spiked with Sambuca and topped with whipped cream, as is sometimes done in Sicily, where granita making is an art form, it's a terrific way to beat the heat. SERVES 8 TO 10

. INGREDIENTS .

9 cups cold brewed espresso or very strong coffee
5 to 6 tablespoons superfine sugar
1/2 cup Sambuca

1 cup heavy whipped cream
2 teaspoons ground cinnamon

1. In a large bowl, combine the espresso and sugar, stirring until the sugar dissolves. Add the Sambuca and taste. If the mixture doesn't have a sweet taste, add more sugar. To freeze, pour into a 3-quart rectangular stainless-steel baking pan. Place the pan in the freezer and stir every 20 minutes with a balloon whisk. Continue freezing and stirring until the granita is uniformly slushy. This should take about 2 hours; however, the colder your freezer, the faster it will get slushy. Freeze for another 30 minutes before serving, but do not let the granita harden into a solid mass; it should be grainy.

2. Fill goblets two-thirds of the way with the granita, top with whipped cream, and sprinkle with cinnamon.

PASSOVER FLOURLESS CHOCOLATE CAKE

FROM JO-ANN MAKOVITZKY *OF* TOCQUEVILLE

Before Marco Moreira and his wife, Jo-Ann Makovitzky, opened their intimate French-American restaurant Tocqueville, they ran a successful Manhattan catering company, and every year they continue to cater gourmet Passover seders. One reason for the return business is this flourless chocolate cake, a not-so-distant cousin of that ubiquitous molten chocolate confection that oozed its luscious way from one New York dessert menu to the next. For additional depth of flavor, add a dash of Grand Marnier, and even if you don't observe Passover, don't dream of passing up this nondenominational dessert. NOTE: If this is not being made for Passover, butter can be substituted for the margarine. The cake is better made a day in advance to allow the flavors to marry and can even be frozen. For a fudgier center, underbake it. Do not overbeat the egg whites, as they will become difficult to fold into the chocolate, and the cake will be dry. SERVES 8

.INGREDIENTS.

CAKE
11 ounces bittersweet chocolate, broken up
5 ½ ounces (1 stick plus 3 tablespoons)
    kosher margarine
2 tablespoons Grand Marnier or
    other orange liqueur
6 eggs, separated

1 egg white
1 cup sugar

GARNISH
1 pint blueberries or raspberries
1 pint strawberries
1 tablespoon sugar
1 tablespoon Grand Marnier or other orange liqueur

1. CAKE: Preheat the oven to 350° F.

2. Grease a 10-inch round springform pan, and line the bottom with parchment or waxed paper. Place the chocolate and margarine in a metal bowl, and set over a pan of simmering water. When it's melted, stir in the liqueur. Set aside in a warm place.

3. In a bowl, beat the egg yolks together with ½ cup of the sugar until the mixture turns lemon-yellow. In another bowl, beat the 7 egg whites together; when soft peaks form, add the remaining ½ cup of sugar, and beat until medium peaks form.

4. Fold the egg-yolk mixture into the chocolate; then fold in the egg whites, a third at a time. Pour the batter into the prepared pan and bake for 20 minutes. Reduce the oven temperature to 300° F and bake for another 20 minutes. Reduce the oven temperature to 250° F and bake for another 50 minutes, or until a toothpick inserted in the center comes out clear. Allow the cake to cool in the pan, and then remove.

5. GARNISH: Clean and cut the berries to desired size. Toss in a bowl with the sugar and liqueur, and allow to sit for 10 minutes.

6. To serve, slice the cake into eight pieces. Spoon some berry mixture gently over each slice.

BUTTERSCOTCH PUDDING

FROM MELISSA MURPHY *OF* DROVERS TAP ROOM

Were you to take a poll, you'd probably find that everyone's favorite pudding is chocolate, but not everyone has tried Melissa Murphy's butterscotch version. Everyone should. Murphy, who was the pastry chef at the short-lived Drovers Tap Room, a sister restaurant to David Page's comfort-food mecca, Home, moved on to open her own charming Cobble Hill, Brooklyn, bakeshop, Sweet Melissa Patisserie, where she still serves this irresistible, homey dessert. What distinguishes Murphy's pudding is an exquisite balance of salty-sweet flavors and a gorgeous crème-caramel texture. One bite and you'll be a butterscotch convert for life. NOTE: To stop a skin from forming on the individual puddings, press a piece of plastic wrap directly onto the surface. They can be kept in the refrigerator for up to 2 days. SERVES 6

·INGREDIENTS·

6 egg yolks
¼ cup packed dark brown sugar
1 cup milk
2 cups heavy cream

¾ cup granulated sugar
1 teaspoon salt
1 teaspoon vanilla extract

1. Preheat the oven to 300° F.

2. Place the egg yolks in a large bowl and whisk gently until smooth. Set aside.

3. Heat the brown sugar, milk, and cream in a saucepan until the sugar starts to dissolve, then heat to the scalding point (do not boil). Remove from the heat; cover to keep warm.

4. In a small saucepan, combine the granulated sugar with ¼ cup of water and bring to a boil. If the sugar starts to spatter, use a pastry brush dipped in water to wash down the sides of the saucepan. As soon as the sugar turns amber, carefully add ¼ cup of the hot cream mixture, whisking until combined. Whisk in 2 more cups of the cream mixture, then add the rest.

5. Pour the caramel cream into the yolks in a thin stream, whisking the mixture continuously. Strain through a sieve into a bowl, add the salt and vanilla, and place the bowl in an ice bath, stirring to cool. Skim any foam from the surface and pour the caramel cream into six 5-ounce ramekins, leaving ½ inch at the top of each. Place the ramekins in a shallow roasting pan and fill the pan with hot water to come halfway up their sides. Cover with foil.

6. Bake for about 1¼ hours, or until the puddings are set. (When one is shaken, the center should look a little loose. The cooking time will vary depending on the temperature of the hot water added to the roasting pan.) Remove from the oven; allow to cool in the hot water. Cover each ramekin with plastic and refrigerate for 3 hours or overnight.

CANDIED WALNUT TART

FROM WAYNE NISH *OF* MARCH

If you've had one too many overly sweet pecan pies at Thanksgiving, it might be time for a new nut. Wayne Nish's signature candied walnut tart is as simple as taking your favorite tart shell, filling it with walnuts that have been tossed together with brown sugar, butter, honey, and cream, then baking the whole thing together until the walnut flavor intensifies. That makes it as easy as it is delicious—an important holiday consideration.

SERVES 6 TO 8

. INGREDIENTS .

4 ounces (1 stick) unsalted butter
¾ cup light brown sugar
2 tablespoons granulated sugar
¼ cup honey

¼ cup heavy cream
1 pound walnut pieces
1 prebaked 9-inch tart shell

1. Preheat the oven to 325° F.

2 . Melt the butter and sugars in a saucepan over medium heat; add the honey, and cook until the mixture reaches 250° F on a candy thermometer. Remove from the heat, add the cream and nuts, and stir to mix thoroughly.

3. Pour the walnuts into the tart shell, and bake until the center of the filling is bubbling, about 20 minutes. Serve warm with vanilla ice cream. The tart will keep for a week at room temperature (do not refrigerate).

LEMON SOUFFLÉ TART

FROM LEN ALLISON *OF* HUBERTS

In its late-eighties prime, Huberts was a culinary trendsetter and an incubator of young cooking talent, where chef-partner Len Allison avidly explored the shifting parameters of New American cuisine. In this recipe, he seamlessly transforms the classic American lemon meringue pie into an elegant lemon soufflé tart that enjoys the textural advantages of soufflé without its downside (the looming threat of imminent collapse). Unlike the traditional tyrannical soufflé, which must be slavishly served the instant it emerges from the oven, this tart can be made ahead of time, at your leisure, and served at room temperature. Now that's what we call progress. SERVES 8

. INGREDIENTS .

8 eggs, separated
²/₃ cup sugar
Zest of 1 lemon, grated
1 tablespoon all-purpose flour
Juice of 4 lemons

1 tablespoon unsalted butter, softened
Pinch salt
Pinch cream of tartar
One 10-inch tart shell, baked and
   glazed with egg white

1. Preheat the oven to 400° F.

2. Using an electric mixer, beat the egg yolks with ¹/₃ cup of sugar, the lemon zest, and the flour until thick and pale yellow.

3. Transfer to a double boiler and add the lemon juice. Whisk over medium heat until thick and set. Remove from the heat and whisk in the butter. Cover and set aside.

4. Using an electric mixer, beat the egg whites with salt and cream of tartar until they form soft peaks. Add the remaining ¹/₃ cup of sugar, and beat until firm peaks form. By hand, whisk one third of the egg whites into the yolk mixture. Using a rubber spatula, fold in the remaining whites.

5. Mound the mixture in the tart shell, and bake for 15 to 18 minutes, rotating the pan 180 degrees after 9 minutes. Let cool before serving.

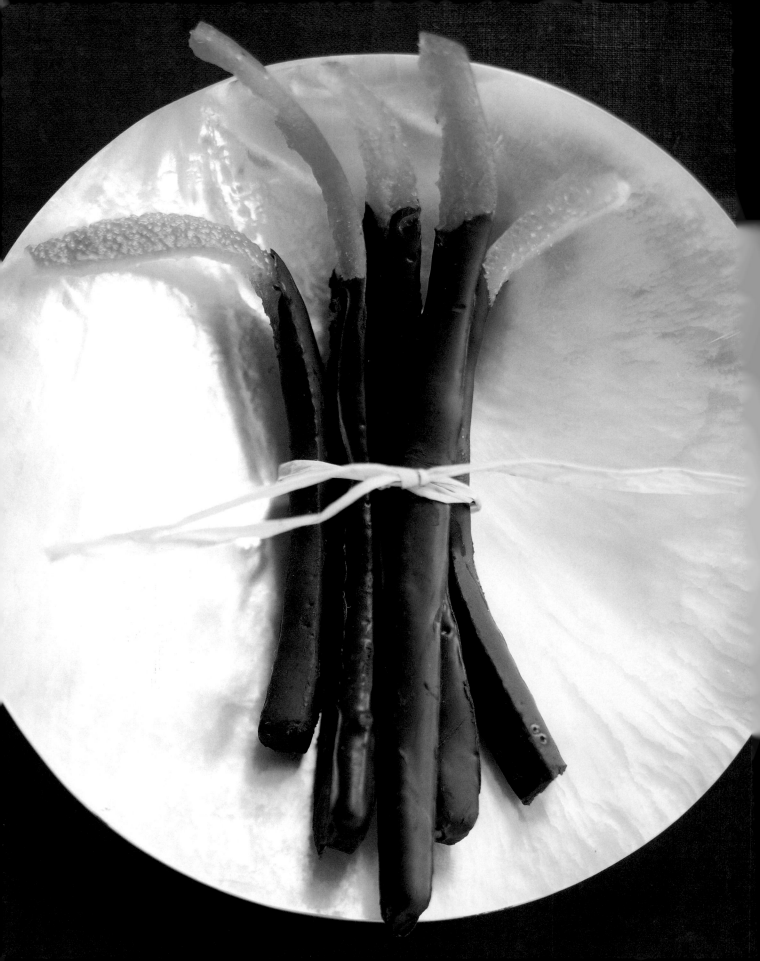

CHOCOLATE-DIPPED CANDIED CITRUS

FROM FRANÇOIS PAYARD *OF* PAYARD PATISSERIE

François Payard might not have been born with a silver spoon in his mouth, but with his parents running a traditional patisserie in Nice, chances are he had something rich and delicious to chew on. In 1997 he left his position as pastry chef at Restaurant Daniel to open his own patisserie and bistro on the Upper East Side, where well-heeled neighbors convene for freshly baked croissants, spectacular pastries, and a mouthwatering assortment of candy. For our special issue featuring edible holiday gifts, François volunteered this recipe for chocolate-dipped candied orange peel. Make a large batch, since it will keep for several months if refrigerated in its syrup. François suggests tempering the chocolate before dipping the peel, to prevent a bloom from developing over the course of several days. If only they lasted that long! NOTE: The candied peel can be chopped and added to fruit cakes and candies or used as a garnish. If you don't feel like dipping the peel in chocolate, it can be rolled in a little sugar and left to dry. YIELDS 3 TO 5 DOZEN.

. INGREDIENTS .

1 orange
1 lemon
1 lime
1 grapefruit

2 1/3 cups sugar
4 tablespoons light corn syrup
12 ounces bittersweet chocolate (preferably Valrhona or Callebaut), finely chopped

1. TO PREPARE THE PEEL: Slice each fruit in half, squeeze out the juice, and remove and discard the pulp. In a medium saucepan, stir together the sugar, corn syrup, and 4 cups of water. Bring to a boil. Add the citrus peels, and place a saucer on top to keep them submerged. Cook for 5 hours just below the boiling point. (Use a flame tamer to keep the temperature down.) After 5 hours, the syrup will be twice as thick as when you began. Transfer the peel and syrup to a bowl, and set in the refrigerator overnight. (Candied peel will keep in the syrup for one year.)

2. Drain the peel, scrape out most of the pith, and cut into 1/4-inch strips. Dry on a rack for 2 to 3 hours. (They must be thoroughly dry before you begin dipping.)

3. TO TEMPER THE CHOCOLATE: Melt 8 ounces of the chocolate in a bowl placed over simmering water, until the temperature reaches 110° F (it will feel warm when touched to the lips). Remove the bowl of chocolate from the heat, and dry the bottom. Using a spatula, stir in the remaining chocolate. When it has all melted and no lumps remain, return the bowl to the simmering water, and heat for 3 to 5 seconds, until the chocolate feels warm on the lips again. Remove from the heat.

4. TO COAT: Dip each fruit strip into the chocolate, coating three-quarters of the strip, and place on a parchment-lined cookie sheet. Reheat the chocolate over the hot water if it cools and stiffens. Allow the dipped citrus to set in the refrigerator for about 30 minutes.

CONVERSION CHARTS

WEIGHT EQUIVALENTS The metric weights given in this chart are not exact equivalents, but have been rounded up or down slightly to make measuring easier.

VOLUME EQUIVALENTS These are not exact equivalents for American cups and spoons, but have been rounded up or down slightly to make measuring easier.

AVOIRDUPOIS	METRIC
¼ oz	7 g
½ oz	15 g
1 oz	30 g
2 oz	60 g
3 oz	90 g
4 oz	115 g
5 oz	150 g
6 oz	175 g
7 oz	200 g
8 oz (½ lb)	225 g
9 oz	250 g
10 oz	300 g
11 oz	325 g
12 oz	350 g
13 oz	375 g
14 oz	400 g
15 oz	425 g
16 oz (1 lb)	450 g
1½ lb	750 g
2 lb	900 g
2¼ lb	1 kg
3 lb	1.4 kg
4 lb	1.8 kg

AMERICAN	METRIC		IMPERIAL
¼ t	1.2 ml		
½ t	2.5 ml		
1 t	5.0 ml		
½ T (1.5 t)	7.5 ml		
1 T (3 t)	15 ml		
¼ cup (4 T)	60 ml		2 fl oz
⅓ cup (5 T)	75 ml		2½ fl oz
⅓ cup (8 T)	125 ml	4 fl oz	
⅔ cup (10 T)	150 ml	5 fl oz	
¾ cup (12 T)	175 ml	6 fl oz	
1 cup (16 T)	250 ml		8 fl oz
1¼ cups	300 ml		10 fl oz (½ pt)
1½ cups	350 ml		12 fl oz
2 cups (1 pint)	500 ml		16 fl oz
2½ cups	625 ml		20 fl oz (1 pint)
1 quart	1 liter		32 fl oz

OVEN TEMPERATURE EQUIVALENTS

OVEN MARK	F	C	GAS
Very cool	250–275	130–140	½–1
Cool	300	150	2
Warm	325	170	3
Moderate	350	180	4
Moderately hot	375	190	5
	400	200	6
Hot	425	220	7
	450	230	8
Very hot	475	250	9

RECIPE INDEX

CHEF AND RESTAURANT INDEX